THE GREEK OF THE FOURTH GOSPEL

THE UNIVERSITY OF CHICAGO PRESS
CHICAGO, ILLINOIS

———

THE BAKER & TAYLOR COMPANY
NEW YORK

THE CAMBRIDGE UNIVERSITY PRESS
LONDON

THE MARUZEN-KABUSHIKI-KAISHA
TOKYO, OSAKA, KYOTO, FUKUOKA, SENDAI

THE GREEK
OF
THE FOURTH GOSPEL

A STUDY OF
ITS ARAMAISMS IN THE LIGHT OF
HELLENISTIC GREEK

By

ERNEST CADMAN COLWELL

THE UNIVERSITY OF CHICAGO PRESS
CHICAGO, ILLINOIS

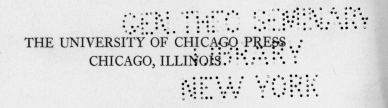

TO
ANNETTE CARTER COLWELL

PREFACE

The pens of scholars who are authorities on Aramaic and Hebrew usage have been compiling for the last eight years an ever lengthening list of "Semitic constructions" in the Greek of the Fourth Gospel. For most of these constructions the claim is made that they are "un-Greek" or "impossible as Greek"; but no thoroughgoing attempt to evaluate them as Greek has yet been made. It is the purpose of the present work to make such an evaluation by interrogating the non-literary papyri and the *Discourses* of Epictetus on the constructions involved.

That this study has been made at all is due to the suggestion and encouragement of Professor E. J. Goodspeed, Chairman of the Department of New Testament and Early Christian Literature in the University of Chicago, whose advice has been invaluable at every stage of its development.

The limitations of the work may well seem in some instances to be arbitrary; but limitation of some sort, both in the number of locutions studied and in the areas of Greek literature in which they were observed, was a pragmatic necessity. The number of the "Aramaisms" found in John is being increased with every click of the linotype machine, as is also the number of attacks on these "Aramaisms" by reviewers. The reviews, therefore, have not been especially noticed except as they contributed illustrations of Greek usage. But attention should perhaps be called to a review of Professor Burney's book, *The Aramaic Origin of the Fourth Gospel*, by the Aramaic scholar Gustav Dalman in the *Theologische Literaturzeitung*, Volume XLVIII (1923).

Of all the limitations of his work, the author is fully aware; but it is his hope that the material here presented will make possible a more sane and intelligent estimate of the character of the Greek of the Fourth Gospel than that which is so often advanced today.

To the Rev. Dr. W. F. Howard, of Birmingham, England, the author wishes to express his thanks for the loan of a copy of Dr. S. R. Driver's fine study of Burney's work. And to Dean Shailer Mathews and the Editorial Committee of the Divinity School, the author's thanks are due for making the publication of this study possible.

ERNEST CADMAN COLWELL

CHICAGO, ILLINOIS
June 26, 1931

CONTENTS

CHAPTER   PAGE

I. INTRODUCTION 1

II. SEMITIC IDIOMS IN SENTENCE STRUCTURE 10

III. THE PARTS OF SPEECH 46

IV. MISTRANSLATIONS 96

V. CONCLUSIONS 123

INDEXES 133

ix

CHAPTER I

INTRODUCTION

Was the Fourth Gospel written in Jesus' own language?
Is our Greek gospel a translation from an Aramaic original? Or did its author think in Aramaic while writing in
Greek? These questions are attracting considerable attention on the part of New Testament scholars at the
present time. Many scholars answer one or other in the
affirmative, and several recent works on John assume that
no other answer is possible. Yet there is no dearth of
scholars who advance more or less lengthy negative answers, so that a complete bibliography of recent studies
in this field would be a long one.

But interest in this question is not a phenomenon of
recent appearance. Before the nineteenth century at
least three scholars claimed that the Greek of the Fourth
Gospel was very Semitic, and at the beginning of that
century the same opinion was somewhat elaborated by
L. Berthold.[1] Yet it is not until the beginning of the
present century that we find an extensive development
of the theory. At that time A. Schlatter[2] paralleled many
verses throughout John with material found in the New
Hebrew of Mechilta, Sifre, and other Rabbinic commentaries, the extent to which this could be done convinc-

[1] A brief survey of these earlier studies is given by Burney, *Aramaic Origin of the Fourth Gospel* (Oxford, 1922), pp. 2-3, n.

[2] *Die Sprache und Heimat d. vierten Evangelisten* (Gütersloh, 1902).

I

ing him that the Gospel of John was written by one who thought and spoke in Aramaic. About the same time, Dalman was expressing the opinion that the evidence was not sufficient to show that a written Aramaic gospel ever existed, and he also claimed that the Fourth Gospel was decidedly less Aramaic than the Synoptics.[1] Wellhausen supported the latter conclusion, holding that the Greek of John differs from that of Mark in that it is not disguised Aramaic.[2] The next year, however, saw the plea for a written Aramaic original advanced by C. J. Ball in a brief study of some peculiarities in the language of the Fourth Gospel.[3]

This article stimulated the late C. F. Burney to a study of the language of John which resulted in the most comprehensive argument for an Aramaic original that has appeared up to the present time.[4] His work contains a preliminary testing of the theory by examination of the Prologue, which is "retranslated" into Aramaic; a discussion of Aramaisms in sentence structure, and in the use of conjunctions, pronouns, verbs, and negatives; a series of alleged mistranslations of the original Aramaic of the gospel; an argument that the Old Testament quotations were originally made in Hebrew; and an appendix which reconsiders authorship, place of writing, date, etc., in the light of the Aramaic original. He insists (pp. 7 f.)

[1] *The Words of Jesus* (Edinburgh, 1902).

[2] *Das Evangelium Johannis* (Berlin, 1908), p. 145.

[3] "Had the Fourth Gospel an Aramaic Archetype?" *Expository Times*, Vol. XXI (1909).

[4] *Op. cit.*

on the "clear distinction between Aramaisms and Hebraisms," but nevertheless uses Hebraisms (pp. 96, etc.)
as an argument for the Aramaic original. As the basis for
his linguistic argument, the assumption is made that the
Synoptic Gospels are standard Koine Greek. And Aramaisms in John are, for the most part, detected by a
quantitative comparison of the usage of John with their
usage, the relative frequency or infrequency of Synoptic
usage in John indicating the Aramaism. For example,
John uses ἵνα μή three times as frequently as the Synoptists do, and since this "over-use" departs from Synoptic
usage—that is, from Greek usage—it must be an Aramaism. The establishment of mistranslations he regards
as essential to his argument, and claims that his mistranslations must be so classified because of difficulties and
peculiarities of language.

At the same time that Burney was working out his
theory, James A. Montgomery was independently arriv-
ing at a similar conclusion. In his short study of the origin of John[1] he discusses geographical and historical data,
data bearing on Jewish institutions, the Aramaic background of the gospel, and its theology. His argument for
the Aramaic background does not demand a *written* Aramaic original; nor does he ordinarily establish the Aramaism by contrasting John with the Synoptists—he
notes, rather, those cases which seem to him to represent
Aramaic constructions. The demonstration of mistranslations is not, therefore, necessary to his thesis; and he
prefaces his list of "possible" evidences for a written

[1] *The Origin of the Gospel According to St. John* (Philadelphia, 1923).

Aramaic original with a word of caution which calls attention to this fact.

Soon after its appearance, Burney's work was reviewed by C. C. Torrey,[1] who summarizes previous pleas for an Aramaic original of John and carries the argument on. He confesses that the main body of Burney's work seems convincing to him, although he rejects the mistranslations for which Burney argues, almost without exception, and is willing to admit Hellenistic influence in the "logos" and the mysticism of the Fourth Gospel. His contribution lies in suggesting the Aramaic nature of several Johannine constructions to which attention had been called by Wellhausen, and in supplying a new set of mistranslations to replace those of Burney which he has rejected. His indorsement of Burney's main argument is remarkable in view of the fact that he regards the Synoptic Gospels as retaining more traces of Semitic origin and influence than John, whereas Burney's argument rests largely upon establishing John's usage as a contrast to Synoptic usage.

Among the many reviews of Burney's work, the three most important are those of Allis,[2] Driver,[3] and Howard.[4] These present Greek parallels to many of the Aramaisms

[1] "The Aramaic Origin of the Gospel of John," *Harvard Theological Review*, XVI (1923), 305–44.

[2] "The Alleged Aramaic Origin of the Fourth Gospel," *Princeton Theological Review*, XXVI (1928), 531–72.

[3] "The Original Language of the Fourth Gospel," *Jewish Guardian*, January 5, 12, 1923.

[4] Moulton and Howard, *Grammar of New Testament Greek* (Edinburgh, 1929), II, 413–85.

claimed by Burney; but while they deny the existence of an Aramaic Gospel of John, they incline toward the idea that the author of the Fourth Gospel had an Aramaic source, probably oral, for the words of Jesus. Professor Howard's work is embodied in an appendix ("Semitisms in the New Testament") to the second volume of his grammar, the most comprehensive and thoroughgoing treatment of this subject that has yet appeared.

These reviews, in turn, have been used by Professor Millar Burrows in the most significant contribution to the study of the hypothesis of an Aramaic original of the Gospel of John which has appeared since Burney's work.[1] The contribution lies not in any fresh study of either Greek or Aramaic background but rather in the classification and evaluation of the Aramaisms discussed by the writers mentioned above. Thus he discusses the possibility of Septuagint influence, of the existence of a "Palestinian" Greek, of the author's thinking in Aramaic, and of actual translation from a written Aramaic original. And under the heading of "Apparent Semitisms" he lists more than a dozen usages which he feels have been justified by the Hellenists' studies as Greek usage. But he still feels (p. 139) that "the almost overwhelming evidence of John's Semitisms and even mistranslations . . . ." makes ". . . . the hypothesis of a Palestinian or Syrian gospel written in Aramaic, with a later Ephesian translation and rescension" seem "entirely probable." This statement, however, like the entire article, lacks

[1] "The Original Language of the Gospel of John," *Journal of Biblical Literature*, XLIX (1930), 95 ff.

that note of dogmatic assurance which weakens previous studies in this field.

The present study is based upon the works of Burney, Montgomery, and Torrey; and large use is made of the valuable material supplied by Allis, Driver, Howard, and Burrows in the articles mentioned above. The Semitisms which these scholars advocate or attack have been established by one of two methods, each of which lacks a label. The first is that of comparative study in Greek. That is to say, the Greek of John is compared with "normal" Greek, and what is different is claimed as an Aramaism. Thus, if a Johannine usage does not appear in "normal" Greek, it is an Aramaism; or the difference may be one of quantity only; thus John may use a certain Greek construction five times as often as it is used in "normal" Greek, the explanation being that this construction is very frequent in Aramaic. J. H. Moulton himself claims that "the over-use of locutions which can be defended as good *Koine* Greek" is an evidence of Semitic influence, a decision which has been taken up by Burney and is fundamental to his method.[1] Not a word can be said against this in theory; in its application the all-important thing is the selection of the basis for normal use and the determination of possible variation within this normal Greek usage. This basis Burney finds in Synoptic usage, and he regards it as so normative that at times only a slight variation from it is used as evidence for an Aramaism in John. Yet on other occasions (e.g.,

[1] *Cambridge Biblical Essays*, p. 474, quoted by Burney, *op. cit.*, pp. 7, 57, cf. W. E. Barnes, *Journal of Theological Studies*, XXIII (1923), 419.

p. 17) the agreement of John with Mark is regarded as a strong argument for the Aramaic original of John, since Mark is the work "of a Palestinian Jew who either actually wrote in Aramaic, or whose mind was so moulded by Aramaic idiom that his Greek perforce reflected it." It would seem, then, that where Mark agrees with John it is Aramaic; where it differs from John, it is Greek. Luke (p. 9) is the "most Hebraic gospel of the four"; and Mathew (p. 8, n.) is either directly or through his sources influenced by Aramaic. If the Synoptic Gospels are so Semitic, they make an unsatisfactory standard by which to measure the language of John.

The second method of establishing Aramaisms in John may be called the "Aramaic comparative method." Thus, if a certain construction "looks Semitic" or if a phrase reminds the investigator of a phrase in Semitic literature from the Assuan papyri to the Talmud, the explanation is that the construction or phrase is an Aramaism. In this method there is usually no attempt to check up by comparison with Greek usage. But the value of such a check on Aramaisms, however established, is shown by Burrows' admission (p. 98) that where the usages of the Fourth Gospel are equally common in the colloquial Greek of the period, the expressions in question cease to have any value as evidence of translation.

To secure a contemporary, neutral, non-Semitic control for Johannine usage, I have turned to the papyri of the Roman period and the *Discourses* of Epictetus.[1] The

---

[1] H. Schenkl, *Epicteti Dissertationes ab Arriano Digestae, Editio Maior* (Leipzig, 1916).

Discourses were included in this study as being one of the
least Semitic of John's contemporaries; for, though New
Testament constructions in the papyri have been explained by some as due to the influence of the Jewish
language upon the Egyptian Koine, no such influence
upon Epictetus has yet been predicated. But it should
not be inferred that the writings of Epictetus and the
papyri have been regarded as furnishing a fixed standard
for Hellenistic Greek usage from which there is no devia-
tion; the wide variation in the usage of individual writers
among the Greeks is a factor which must be taken into
consideration in any study of this sort.

The method employed has been to make a list of the
constructions in John which Burney, Montgomery, or
Torrey regarded as Aramaisms, and to look for these
same constructions in the papyri and the *Discourses*.
Since there is little duplication in the three lists of Aramaisms, it was felt necessary to limit the study to some
extent. As the most easily detached parts of Burney's
work are the preliminary study of the Prologue, and the
argument on the original language of the Old Testament
quotations, these have not been dealt with, as such, in
this work. Yet many of the passages in the Prologue
which Burney recognized as Aramaisms have been discussed under the head of mistranslations or in connection
with similar constructions elsewhere in the gospel.

No confidence is felt that the evidence of either the
Discourses or the papyri has been presented in anything
approaching exhaustive fashion. The number of locutions involved, as well as the extent of the field covered,

makes it certain that many another parallel besides those listed here may be drawn from the *Discourses* and the papyri that have been studied, as also from the large number of published papyri which have not been used in this connection. Still less is any claim for completeness advanced for the testimony of classical Greek. Its use is more or less incidental, and it was included only because it reduces to an absurdity the claim that a construction which it supports "is impossible as Greek." Even more incidental is the occasional use of modern Greek parallels.

But the author feels more apologetic for his occasional use of statistics and approximate totals than for the incompleteness of their presentation. Where they are used, it is not from any undue confidence in the power of figures to settle linguistic disputes, but rather to meet the figures presented by Dr. Burney. Nowhere are statistics more misleading than in the attempt to reduce to order the wide variety of Greek usage; and the figures presented here will, it is hoped, discourage future attempts to find large significance in small variation.

CHAPTER II

SEMITIC IDIOMS IN SENTENCE STRUCTURE

1. ASYNDETON

The frequency of asyndeton in Aramaic as opposed to Hebrew leads Burney[1] to the conclusion that the frequency of asyndeton in John is an evidence of its Aramaic origin. In John, chapter 1, neglecting openings in speeches, he finds 34 asyndeton and 28 connected sentences; in John, chapter 11, 59 sentences with 17 asyndeton; in John, chapter 18, 52 sentences with 20 asyndeton. This proportion, he points out, is very high as compared with the Synoptics: Matthew, chapter 3, contains 13 sentences, no asyndeton; Luke, chapter 8, contains 60 sentences, 2 asyndeton; Mark, chapter 1, contains 38 sentences, 2 asyndeton. Burrows[2] lists John's asyndeton with Aramaisms which may be due to thinking in Aramaic.

There is no other phase of linguistic argument where figures are less significant than they are in this case. In the first place, the unit of measurement is an elusive quantity; it has been impossible to count the instances of asyndeton in John, chapter 1, so as to get figures that would agree with Burney's. If independent, co-ordinate

[1] Burney, *Aramaic Origin of the Fourth Gospel,* pp. 50 f.

[2] Burrows, "The Original Language of the Gospel of John," *Journal of Biblical Literature*, XLIX, 112.

clauses are counted as sentences, the proportion of asyndeton perceptibly decreases; Burney himself notes (p. 40)
in regard to the Prologue "its fondness for co-ordination
of sentences linked by καί." However, in John, chapters
2–4, 11, 18, and 19, a count of the independent co-ordinate clauses gives the totals, 130 asyndeton, 274 syndeton. It is, therefore, true that asyndeton is much more
common in John than it is in the first three gospels. Does
this differentiate John from Hellenistic Greek?

In a count of syndeton and asyndeton sentences in
approximately 200 papyri of the Roman period, 22 were
found with no connected sentences at all. Several of these
consist of only 2 sentences; but one, P. Fay, 117 (letter,
108 A.D.), contains 8 asyndeton sentences; another, P.
Oxy, III, 466 (directions for wrestling, ii A.D.), although
it consists almost entirely of imperatives, contains 13.
There are many more in which unconnected sentences
far outnumber those with connectives; e.g., P. Oxy. I,
113 (letter, ii A.D.), 10 asyndeton, 1 syndeton; P. Lond.
II, 265 (instructions for converting artabae, i A.D.), 91
asyndeton, 25 syndeton. On the other hand, equally
weighty examples might be cited for the prevalence of
connected sentences in the papyri; for between papyri,
as between gospels, there is wide variation in usage.

In the *Discourses* of Epictetus a count of asyndeton
and syndeton sentences is rather difficult. The frequency
of fragmentary sentences and the rapid dialogue make it
difficult to secure definite and exact results. Thus, in a
count of i. 14 to i. 24, inclusive, 244 asyndeton sentences
were found to 220 syndeton. If a high degree of accuracy

were essential, some further counting would be necessary; but the most careful checking would still leave Epictetus much closer to John than to the Synoptic Gospels.

There is very little narrative in Epictetus, but the occasional narratives in his teaching have a very high percentage of unconnected sentences; e.g., i. 18. 13 f.: ἔχεις καλὰ ἱμάτια, ὁ γείτων σου οὐκ ἔχει· θυρίδα ἔχεις, θέλεις αὐτὰ ψῦξαι. οὐκ οἶδεν ἐκεῖνος τί τὸ ἀγαθόν ἐστι τοῦ ἀνθρώπου, ἀλλὰ φαντάζεται ὅτι τὸ ἔχειν κτλ. Compare also i. 19. 24 f. Asyndeton occurs more frequently in such passages than in the narrative sections of John. A count of the narrative sections in John, chapters 2–4, 11, 18, and 19, gives 17 asyndeton against 162 connected sentences, the proportion in the last three chapters being much less than one in ten.

In the same six chapters, however, within the speeches, there were only 62 connected sentences to 59 asyndeton— a much higher proportion. But this is almost exactly the proportion that exists in the *Discourses;* e.g., in i. 14–24, 212 asyndeton to 216 syndeton. A striking example of the extent to which the Stoic preacher carried the use of asyndeton in speeches occurs in i. 17. 20–29, where he dramatically sets forth the reply of the philosopher-soothsayer to an inquirer's appeal. Sentence follows sentence without connective; asyndeton occurs 13 times (aside from the opening of speeches), and only 6 sentences are connected. Thus it is easy to conclude that in the proportion of asyndeton to syndeton sentences, John stands with Epictetus apart from the Synoptics. W. E. Barnes, who quotes in this connection the opening of

Tacitus' *Annals*, is stating the case conservatively when he says, "Asyndeton is far too common a feature of language in general to bear the stress which Dr. Burney lays upon it."[1]

a) ASYNDETON WITH ἀποκρίνομαι

This construction occurs 65 times in John, as against 11 uses of the same verb with connectives, and is found only once outside John in the New Testament. Burney (pp. 52 f.) regards this as due to the asyndeton use of "answered" in Aramaic. His argument runs as follows: 28 instances of "answer" used asynedeton are found in the six Aramaic chapters of Daniel, against 2 cases in which "then" is used as connective. The syndeton use is the rule in Hebrew. Theodotion represents ענה by ἀποκρίνομαι 12 times, preserving the asyndeton 4 times. In 38 passages in John, ἀποκρίνομαι introduces the words spoken without further verb; in the 26 other Johannine cases, καὶ εἶπεν is added. "It is difficult," says Burney (p. 54), "to resist the conclusion that ἀπεκρίθη καὶ εἶπεν (and the plural form) is a literal rendering of the Aramaic ענה ואמר . . . . for which, as we have seen, they stand in Theodotion's Daniel."

Theodotion's evidence is capable of quite another emphasis than that given by Burney. In the first place, he omits the verb "answer" 16 times. In the next place, he uses it without εἶπεν only once. Of the 12 asyndeton passages in which he translates ענה, 8 are made syndeton in his Greek. That is to say, if a predominance of asyndeton

---

[1] *Journal of Theological Studies*, XXIII (1923), 419.

in the use of ἀποκρίνομαι were used as a test of Greek
translated from Aramaic, Theodotion's translation of the
Aramaic would give a negative result! The worthlessness
of this test for an Aramaic original has been indicated
further by Bernard, who points out that it "is common in
the Septuagint, where the original is Hebrew (not Aramaic), e.g., I Sam. 14:28; 19:22; II Chron. 29:31; 34:15;
Joel 2:19 (of Jahweh)."[1] Thus the fact that ἀποκρίνομαι
is used without connectives in John needs no Aramaic
idiom to support it.[2] But the use of the entire phrase
ἀπεκρίθη καὶ εἶπεν in John is undoubtedly due to Semitic
influence of some kind. Burney doubtless avoided stress-
ing it because it is not distinctively Aramaic; in fact,
Dalman claims that true Aramaic probably did not know
this formula, and that the Evangelists must have taken
it either direct from the Hebrew or indirectly through
the Septuagint.[3] In the case of John, a third possibility
is influence of the Synoptics.

b) Asyndeton with λέγω

Burney (pp. 54 f.) finds this usage more common in
John (70 times as against syndeton λέγω 31 times) than in
the Synoptic Gospels (Matthew, 26; Mark, 1; Luke, 2).
He regards it as a translation of the asyndeton אמר participle, which, though not found in Daniel, was yet common in Aramaic in John's day, especially in its eastern
branch. He parallels John 21:15–17 with a passage taken
from the Syriac *Acts of Thomas*, and claims (p. 56) that

[1] *St. John* (New York, 1928), p. 65.

[2] Cf. the preceding and the following section.

[3] *Die Worte Jesu*[2] (Leipzig, 1930), p. 20.

"the striking resemblance in structure between the two passages . . . . is no mere chance and isolated phenomenon." The explanation of this relationship may be that the *Acts of Thomas* was written originally in Greek, an opinion that is maintained by M. R. James.[1]

My own count of the asyndeton use of all verbs of saying in John 1:19—4:54, and chapters 11, 18, and 19, gives these totals: 71 asyndeton, 70 syndeton. In Epictetus i. 19—ii. 15, λέγω appears asyndeton approximately 44 times, and syndeton about 40 times; φημί, however, in the same passage is used with a connective only 7 out of 25 times. This usage of Epictetus, even if λέγω alone be compared, is much closer to John than to the Synoptic Gospels. The *Discourses* depart from John not so much in the direction of syndeton as in the direction of still greater asyndeton, omitting even the verb of saying; e.g., i. 29. 4–6: καὶ φησίν 'εἴ τι ἀγαθὸν θέλεις, παρὰ σεαυτοῦ λάβε'. σὺ λέγεις 'οὔ· ἀλλὰ παρ' ἄλλου'. μή, ἀλλὰ παρὰ σεαυτοῦ. λοιπὸν ὅταν ἀπειλῇ ὁ τύραννος καὶ μὴ καλῇ, λέγω 'τίνι ἀπειλεῖ;' ἂν λέγῃ 'δήσω σε', φημὶ ὅτι 'ταῖς χερσὶν ἀπειλεῖ καὶ τοῖς ποσίν'. ἂν λέγῃ 'τραχηλοκοπήσω σε', λέγω 'τῷ τραχήλῳ ἀπειλεῖ'. ἂν λέγῃ 'εἰς φυλακήν σε βαλῶ', 'ὅλῳ τῷ σαρκιδίῳ'· κἂν ἐξορισμὸν ἀπειλῇ, τὸ αὐτό.

A close parallel to John's use of λέγω, including the historical present tense, is to be found in Hermas; e.g., Vision 1:3:3: μετὰ τὸ παῆναι αὐτῆς τὰ ῥήματα ταῦτα λέγει μοι· Θέλεις ἀκοῦσαί μου ἀναγινωσκούσης; λέγω κἀγώ· Θέλω, κυρία. λέγει μοι· Γενοῦ ἀκροατὴς . . . . . ; Vision 3:2:4; καὶ ἐπάρασα ῥάβδον τινὰ λαμπρὰν λέγει μοι· Βλέπεις μέγα

---

[1] *The Apocryphal New Testament* (Oxford, 1926), p. 364.

πρᾶγμα; λέγω αὐτῇ· Κυρία, οὐδὲν βλέπω. λέγει μοι· Σύ, ἰδού, οὐχ ὁρᾷς. . . . . Such passages, and the high percentage of asyndeton use of λέγω in Epictetus, weaken the claim advanced by Burney for translation from an Aramaic gospel.

c) Asyndeton Imperatives

Montgomery[1] notices this as a "Semitic-looking" case, and gives as an example John 5:8, "Rise, take up." Burrows (p. 112) also seems to regard this as an evidence that the author was thinking in Aramaic.

That this construction was not unknown in classical Greek is shown by Gildersleeve's casual examples given in another connection: Sophocles *Tr.* 1255, Homer *Iliad* iii. 82.[2]

Its persistence into Hellenistic times is proved by numerous occurrences in the papyri and the *Discourses;* e.g., P. Oxy. I, 33 (report of a trial, ii A.D.), column I, line 11: τρέχε, τέκνον, τελεύτα; and in the same MS, col. III, line 8. Epictetus ii. 7. 13: κύριε, ἐλέησον· ἐπίτρεψόν μοι ἐξελθεῖν. In the same sources, imperative sentences are often construed asyndeton; e.g., P. Oxy. II, 295 (letter, 35 A.D.), line 7: προσδέχου ἰς τὸν ἐνιαυτὸν Λουκία. γράψον μοι τὴν ἡμέραν. ἄσπασαι σὺ 'Αμμωνᾶν. Compare Epictetus i. 25. 8. In P. Lond. II, 265 (instructions for converting artabae, i. A.D.), in which almost every main verb is an imperative, asyndeton occurs 91 out of 116 times. And Epictetus goes far beyond anything found in the Fourth Gospel both in the extent of individual series of asyndeton

[1] *The Origin of the Gospel According to St. John*, p. 16.
[2] *Greek Syntax*, I (New York, 1900), 163, 165.

imperatives and in the frequency with which he employs
the construction; e.g., iii. 21. 5: τοιοῦτόν τι καὶ σὺ ποίησον·
φάγε ὡς ἄνθρωπος, πίε ὡς ἄνθρωπος, κοσμήθητι, γάμησον,
παιδοποίησον, πολίτευσαι· ἀνάσχου λοιδορίας, ἔνεγκε ἀδελφὸν
ἀγνώμονα, ἔνεγκε πατέρα, ἔνεγκε υἱόν, γείτονα, σύνοδον.
Compare 1. 16. 11; 18. 14; 24. 5; 25. 8, 30; 27. 6, 9; 29.
10; ii. 1. 35; 20. 26; iii. 5. 3; 12. 15; 13. 21; 14. 3; 21. 6;
24. 85; 26. 22; iv. 1. 106; 2. 8; 4. 15; 9. 11; 11. 17; 13. 15.
This would seem to indicate that the Greek readers of
John's gospel found nothing unusual in his employment
of an occasional asyndeton imperative.

2. Parataxis

As contrasted with the "general infrequency" of καί
in John, Burney (p. 66) claims that it "is frequent in
John in speeches, linking co-ordinate clauses, as in a
Semitic language." This brief and rather vague statement is the extent of Burney's discussion of this construction; he does not say how frequent it is, nor does he tell
us what the norm is in comparison with which John's use
seems frequent.

καί linking co-ordinate clauses, whether in speeches or
out of them, is too obviously acceptable Greek to need
argument; nor has the construction any distinction, for—
aside from Semitic usage—it is common to practically all
the Indo-European languages. The battle over parataxis
in general as a Semitism has already been fought out.
Howard[1] surveys the battlefield; and Driver agrees with
the conclusion of Radermacher, who, after surveying late

[1] *Grammar of New Testament Greek*, II, 423.

Greek usage, decides that a free and frequent use of καί
was a feature of popular speech in Greek as in Hebrew.[1]

The infrequency of καί in narrative in John is mentioned rather incidentally in this connection by Burney
(p. 66). He quotes from Abbott the totals for the four
gospels, and observes that John's "comparative infrequency seems to be due partly to the writer's use of
asyndeton, partly to his fondness for οὖν." It may be due
in part also to the fact noted elsewhere by Burney that
John has much less narrative than the Synoptic Gospels
have. Since both asyndeton and the frequency of οὖν are
discussed elsewhere in this study, Burney's example is
followed in omitting any discussion of the infrequency
of καί as such.

a) RARITY OF THE AORIST PARTICIPLE

The description of this idiom by Burney (p. 56) merits
quotation: "In speaking above of John's phrase ἀπεκρίθη
καὶ εἶπεν, we noticed that the Synoptic equivalent sub-
ordinates *the prior action*[2] by use of the Aorist Participle;
e.g., ὁ δὲ ἀποκριθεὶς εἶπεν, i.e. the natural Greek construction." He gives statistics to show that such use of the
aorist participle is less than one-fourth as frequent in
John as in the Synoptics. The conclusion which he draws
is that the "over-use" of parataxis in John, which lies
behind the infrequent use of the aorist participle, is an

[1] Radermacher, *Neutestamentliche Grammatik*[2] (Tübingen, 1925),
p. 218.

[2] Italics mine. New Testament grammarians regard this as an aorist
participle of identical action; cf. Burton, *Moods and Tenses* (Chicago,
1898), p. 64.

evidence of the Aramaic original in which parataxis was naturally frequent.

Koine usage was not, however, as standardized, even, as the Synoptic Gospels. Other forces than Semitic influence caused a variation in usage much wider than that cited above. To suggest the extent of this variation, some figures have been compiled on the use of the aorist participle in Epictetus and the papyri. These figures are not worked out in exact detail, but the margin of error that may be included can hardly obliterate their significance.

A count of the aorist participles expressing action prior to the main verb in Epictetus i. 1–11 indicates that they occur about once per Westcott and Hort page. If it were true that half of the instances had been overlooked, the result would still put Epictetus much nearer to the Fourth Gospel than to the others. In about 375 papyri, approximately 88 aorist participles that would come under the category established by Burney were counted. This would represent an average use more infrequent than that of John.

The extent of variability is shown by the fact that in the first 40 papyri studied, the aorist participle occurred but 13 times; yet in one papyrus, P. Oxy. IX, 1188 (official correspondence, 13 A.D.), it occurs 14 times in 29 lines. These figures suggest that an un-Greek rarity of the aorist participle has yet to be established for John.

b) RARITY OF GENITIVE ABSOLUTE

The opinion of the Semitic scholars differs in regard to the use of the genitive absolute in John. Burney (pp.

57 f.) holds that its infrequency as compared with the Synoptists is an evidence of the Semitic original. Torrey, on the other hand (p. 322), will not allow Wellhausen to eliminate the genitive absolute from the *Grundschrift:* "It occurs frequently, however (Burney enumerates 17 cases), and is employed in precisely the manner of the Septuagint." But Burney insists that it is used *infrequently*, the Aramaic equivalent (a temporal clause) having practically displaced it, this clause appearing in John with ὅτε slightly more frequently than in the Synoptic Gospels. Burrows (p. 105) follows Torrey rather than Burney, and claims that "inasmuch as parataxis and temporal clauses were familiar to the early Christians from the Septuagint, Burney's use of them as evidence of translation is inconclusive."

On the question of frequency, it would seem that, so far as the testimony of Epictetus and the papyri is valid, John's use is rather infrequent than frequent. On the basis of i. 1–11, the *Discourses* seem to use the genitive absolute almost twice as frequently as John. And on the basis of 150 instances in 375 papyri, it would seem that the average frequency there is about the same as in the *Discourses*. But between individual papyri there is, of course, the same variability as that noted above in connection with the use of the aorist participle. The same variation occurs in the Apostolic Fathers, a collection of early Christian writings whose origin in Greek has not been questioned. Robinson found a total of 126 genitives absolute in them, and points out the significant fact that they are very unequally divided—The Martyrdom of Polycarp, which is only one twenty-fifth of the whole volume, having one fourth of all the genitives absolute.[1]

Pernot would explain the relative infrequency in John as due to the fact that in that respect his language was closer to the spoken Greek, which today no longer knows the genitive absolute.[2]

Burney also (p. 57) noted a difference in manner of use: "The Synoptists use the construction, almost without exception, in temporal clauses"; while John, he thinks, uses it with a causal meaning in 2:3; 5:13; 6:18, and a concessive force in 12:37; 21:11, and perhaps in 20:19. But these uses have nothing un-Greek in them. Goodwin says that in classical Greek it was used "at first to express time . . . . and afterwards the other circumstantial relations, cause, condition, concession, etc. The construction is most fully developed in Attic prose, especially in the Orators."[3]

3. Position of the Subject
a) Subject after Verb

The position of the subject in John has been attacked in three ways: as usually following the verb, by Torrey; as coming at the end of the sentence, by Montgomery; and particularly, in the case of σύ, as now preceding and now following the verb, by Burney.

Torrey's argument, as the more general, may well be discussed first. It is based on Wellhausen's observations on word-order in John:

[1] *Syntax of the Participle in the Apostolic Fathers* (Chicago, 1913), p. 39.
[2] *Révue des études grecques*, XXXVII (1924), 127.
[3] *Syntax of Moods and Tenses of the Greek Verb* (Boston, 1890), p. 337.

.... thus the verb usually precedes and the subject follows. This seems to agree with Mark and with Semitic usage. But the similarity has this difference: that the subject does not follow the verb directly but seems to prefer the position at the end of the sentence; cf. 2:9; 6:3; 18:33; 19:38. The object, whether it be a noun or pronoun, frequently stands before the subject; and also, frequently, before its verb—especially before the infinitive. John is further differentiated from Mark and Semitic usage by the fact that the genitive (both of nouns and pronouns) often precedes— or is widely separated from—the noun which governs it. . . . . Thus John's word-order is in general un-Semitic, and the precedence of the verb is to be explained as an imitation of biblical style.[1]

Torrey[2] regards this explanation as having no plausibility, "in view of the general character of John's Greek."

A fine review of the discussion of this subject is given by Howard (pp. 416–18), who quotes Lagrange[3] as saying, "this order is Hebrew and Arabic rather than Aramaic and Assyrian (e.g. in Aramaic portions of Daniel the verb more often follows than precedes the subject)."[4] In the same work appears Kiecker's table on the position of the verb in principal clauses in 20 pages of Herodotus, Thucydides, Polybius, The Chronicle of Theophanes, Xenophon, and the gospels. Having made allowance for

[1] Wellhausen, *Das Evangelium Johannis*, pp. 133 f.

[2] "The Aramaic Origin of the Gospel of John," *Harvard Theological Review*, XVI, 323.

[3] *Evangile selon S. Marc* (Paris, 1920), p. lxxxviii.

[4] Professor J. M. Rife of Tarkio College, who is making a study of the word-order of the Greek versions of Daniel, claims that in sentences in which subject, verb, and object are all expressed, the subject usually follows the verbs in Hebrew and precedes in Aramaic.

the fact that the high ratio of verbs in the initial position in the gospels is largely due to the considerable number of verbs of saying, which in accordance with regular Greek usage stand at the beginning of their sentence, Howard still feels that "the predominance of initial position (of the verb) in Luke and John is remarkable."

Some definite figures on word-order are given by Ebeling, who finds, omitting relatives, "that in the *Protagoras* 65% and in the first book of the *Anabasis* 66% of the subjects precede their verbs."[1]

A count of the *Discourses* i. 19–24 indicates that about 78 per cent of Epictetus' subjects precede the verb. But the usage of the papyri seems to be quite different. The relative position of subject and verb in 96 papyri of the Roman period is as follows: subject precedes 123 times, verb precedes 171 times.

Moreover, Wellhausen slightly misrepresented Johannine usage, for the verb does not "usually precede." A count in various chapters of John of all verbs except in relative clauses indicates that the subject precedes in more than 50 per cent of the cases. This percentage is not far removed from those quoted by Ebeling, and is higher than that of the papyri counted in this study.[2] And since John's order agrees with the Hebrew (and the Septuagint) rather than with the Aramaic, it cannot be used as an argument for an Aramaic original of John.

[1] *Gildersleeve Studies* (Baltimore, 1902), p. 238.

[2] The frequency of the order verb–subject in these papyri seems to be due to the formulas of the legal and business papyri, and cannot be emphasized as indicative of Greek word-order in general.

b) SUBJECT AT END OF SENTENCE

Montgomery notes[1] in John "two cases where the subject is thrown apparently without warrant, to the end of the sentence: 3, 24, 'John'; 13, 2, 'Judas', for which I find parallels in Biblical Aramaic and Syriac."

It is interesting to set against this Wellhausen's observation that one of the things that characterized John's word-order as un-Semitic was the fact that the subject does not follow the verb directly but seems to prefer the position at the end of the sentence.[2]

At any rate, whatever the Aramaic order may be, there can be little doubt that Greek word-order was free enough to make a subject at the end of the sentence nothing unusual. It would not be an arduous task to find examples in almost any Greek author; e.g., Plutarch *Greek Questions* (ed. W. R. Halliday) 55, p. 36: καὶ μετὰ ταῦτα πλεύσαντες αὖθις εἰς τὴν νῆσον, ἐκράτησαν τῶν πολεμίων οἱ Σάμιοι.

In the *Discourses* of Epictetus, the subject occurs at the end of the sentence very frequently; e.g., i. 29. 58: ἔστι γὰρ φιλοθεώρόν τι ζῷον ὁ ἄνθρωπος. Compare i. 12. 15, 30; 15. 3; 17. 3; 19. 17, 19, 28; 25. 8, 24, 32; 27. 17; 29. 21, 42; ii. 1. 2; 15. 20; iv. 1. 46, 154, 166, 168, 177; 2. 4; 5. 2, 9, 20; 8. 22, 24; etc.; and P. Lond. II, 328 (live-stock return, 163 A.D.), lines 18 f.

When compared with such examples, the passages in John do not seem convincing evidence of Aramaic influence, even though in them there may seem to be no

---

[1] *Op. cit.*, p. 16.   [2] See above, p. 22.

warrant for putting the subject at the end of the sentence.
The warrant is no stronger in many of the passages cited
above from the *Discourses*.

c) σύ BEFORE AND AFTER VERB

The fact that σύ stands now before and now after the
verb (εἰμί) in John is regarded by Burney (p. 82) as a
striking evidence of agreement with Aramaic idiom,
which could place the pronoun in either position. He cites
1:21*b;* 18:37; 19:9 as examples of the use after the verb
in questions; and 4:19 and 8:48 in statements. The pronoun preceding the verb is found in 1:42, 49; 3:10; 7:52;
etc.; and these passages look to Burney "like a close reproduction of an Aramaic original."

To this Lagrange replies[1] that, aside from the fact
that the Aramaic has no verb to translate,[2] the Greek has
both positions for σύ. He concludes that σύ at the end of
the sentence in John's dialogues is amply justified by the
following examples: Menander *Heros* 6, *Discept.* 324,
Sophocles *Oedipus Rex* 1122.

In the *Discourses*, σύ occurs in both positions with
the copula, in statements and in questions; e.g., in statements: iv. 8. 37: τοιοῦτον εἶ καὶ σὺ φυτάριον· . . . . ; i. 29.
47: σὺ γὰρ ἄξιος εἶ προαχθῆναι μάρτυς ὑπ' ἐμοῦ· . . . . ; and
in questions: iii. 1. 22: 'σὺ οὖν τίς εἶ ;' ... 'σὺ δὲ τίς εἶ ;'
iii. 5. 2: Ἐν οἴκῳ γὰρ ἄνοσος ἦς σύ; In this usage Epictetus
parallels John.

[1] *Évangile selon S. Jean* (Paris, 1925), p. cxiv.

[2] The Septuagint often adds this verb; e.g., Ps. 21:10.

4. Verbal Sequences

a) Imperative and Future Indicative

Three verbal sequences in John have been attacked as evidences of Aramaic influence: the imperative followed by the future indicative, the participle followed by a finite verb, and the aorist followed by an imperfect.

Burney (p. 95) points out that the verbal sequence, imperative and future indicative, is idiomatic in Hebrew, but that it is not so characteristic of Aramaic as it is of Hebrew "except where the sequence is clearly to be regarded as the *result* of the preceding imperative." This, he claims, is the case in the Aramaic of Ezra 7:19–20 and the Greek of John 1:39: Ἔρχεσθε καὶ ὄψεσθε, and 16:24 αἰτεῖτε καὶ λήμψεσθε.

Driver[1] has pointed out that this sequence is classical, occurring "as early as Sophocles (cf. El. 1207 . . . .) while Lucian's *Dial. Deor.* 11. 2 . . . . constitutes an exact parallel."

There can be no doubt as to the prevalence of this construction in the Koine. It is common in the papyri; e.g., P. Oxy. III, 531 (letter, ii A.D.), lines 10 f.: ἀλλὰ τοῖς βιβλίοις σου αὐτὸ μόνον πρόσεχ[ε] φιλολογῶν καὶ ἀπ' αὐτῶν ὄνησιν ἕξεις. Compare P. Oxy. I, 40 (a legal decision, ii/iii A.D.), line 8; P. Fay. 117 (letter, 108 A.D.), line 13; P. Oxy. VI, 886 (magical formula, iii A.D.), lines 20 f.; P. Oxy. X, 1294 (letter, ii/iii A.D.), lines 11 f.

In Epictetus it is more than common: i. 28. 20 (and iv. 1. 51): Ζήτει καὶ εὑρήσεις, ... ii. 2. 20: εἰ γὰρ

---

[1] *Original Language.*

σταυρωθῆναι θέλεις, ἔκδεξαι καὶ ἥξει ὁ σταυρός· . . . . i. 20. 14: ἀνάγνωθι τὰ Ζήνωνος καὶ ὄψει. . . . . In the last example, note that the second verb is ὄψομαι as in John 1:39; it occurs similarly in ii. 8. 25; i. 18. 4; 29. 61; ii. 12. 4, 15; 18. 3; 19. 34; 24. 29; iv. 13. 15. These instances, together with that cited from Lucian by Driver, somewhat weaken the probability that John 1:39 "reflects Jewish usage," as Burrows (p. 116) claims. For examples with other verbs, compare Epictetus i. 4. 15, 29; 15. 5; 19. 28; ii. 1. 35; 2. 25; 16. 20; 19. 20; 20. 4; 22. 9, 10; 26. 7; iii. 9. 22 (twice); 17. 1; 20. 12 (twice); 26. 39; iv. 7. 13, 18. The two instances in John shrink into insignificance when compared with such usage.

b) PARTICIPLE AND FINITE VERB

Burney (pp. 96 f.) calls attention to this construction in John 1:32 and 5:44 as being exactly analogous to a Hebrew idiom of which some examples exist in Aramaic.

The place of the idiom in Greek usage is plainly stated in Winer-Moulton:[1]

The illustrations of anacolouthon which have been given thus far are of such a nature that they might well occur in any language. We have now to mention some particular kinds of anacolouthon which have especially established themselves in Greek usage:— . . . . b. After a participle we often find a transition to the construction with a finite verb. . . . .

It refers to Demosthenes ii. 75, v. 437, 573; Plutarch iv. 323. In Kühner-Gerth[2] much the same statement is made

[1] *Grammar of New Testament Greek*[9] (Edinburgh, 1882), pp. 715 f.

[2] *Ausführliche griechische Grammatik* (Hanover and Leipzig, 1898–1904), § 490, 4.

and numerous examples are given from Homer, Thucydides, Xenophon, and others. Howard (p. 428) calls attention to the citation of nine passages from the *Cyrop.*
by Holden, where this construction occurs; and quotes
Shilleto on Thucydides i. 57, 58 to the effect that the
idiom was very common in Greek.[1] He quotes also (p.
429) as an example of the idiom in Hellenistic Greek,
P. Ryl. II, 153, 40 (138–61 A.D.). Another example from
the papyri is the following: BGU III, 846 (letter, ii A.D.),
lines 13 f.: Ἤκουσα παρὰ το[ῦ Ποστ]ούμου τὸν εὑρόντα σαι
ἐν τῷ Ἀρσινοείτῃ καὶ ἀκαιρίως πάντα σοι διήγηται.

In Epictetus i. 27. 1 participle and finite verb are
plainly co-ordinated as the context shows: ἢ γὰρ ἔστι τινὰ
[καὶ] οὕτως φαίνεται ἢ οὐκ ὄντα οὐδὲ φαίνεται ὅτι ἔστιν ἢ
ἔστι καὶ οὐ φαίνεται ἢ οὐκ ἔστι καὶ φαίνεται. Examples of
this sequence are given from later Greek usage by Jannaris.[2] It would seem, therefore, that the participle co-
ordinated with the finite verb was well established in
Greek usage throughout the history of the language; and
its value as an evidence of Aramaic influence is propor-
tionately weak. Thus Burrows (p. 98) is convinced that
"it cannot be regarded as indicating translation."

c) AORIST AND IMPERFECT

The Hebrew construction with *waw* consecutive has its
counterpart in biblical Aramaic and early Syriac in a sequence of tenses begun with the perfect tense and con-
tinued with participles. And this, Montgomery claims

[1] Cf. also Lagrange, *S. Jean*, p. cvii.

[2] *An Historical Greek Grammar* (London, 1897), § 2168b.

(p. 18), explains why, in John, "the imperfect is constantly cropping up in contrast to the aorists in the neighborhood."

For example, with cases taken at random: "The Jews surrounded (aorist) him and were saying (imperfect) to him," 10, 24; "With a purple robe they clothed him and they were coming and saying," 19, 2; "He went and was asking," 4, 47; the imperfects in 8, 21 ff.

It should be noted in regard to these passages that of the seven imperfects, one is of ἔρχομαι, the other six of verbs of saying, five being ἔλεγε (-ον).

The comment of Kühner-Gerth (§ 383, 3) on such usage in classical Greek is appropriate enough to warrant quotation:

The imperfect was frequently used where one would expect a completed action rather than one still in development, where, therefore, the imperfect seems to stand in place of an aorist. This use occurs especially frequently . . . . in prose with verbs of *sending* and *going* . . . . as well as of *saying*. . . . .

E, 364 f. . . . . ἔβαινε . . . . λάζετο (but δῶκε precedes and μάστιξεν follows). . . . . B, 43 ff. (Impf., Aor., Impf.), H, 303 ff. (Aor., Impf.).

Gildersleeve admits a succession of aorist and imperfect but denies "an actual interchange of tenses."[1] Goodwin says that it was at times a matter of indifference which form was used. "For example," he goes on, "this distinction can seldom be important in such expressions as *he said, he commanded;* and we find ἔλεγον and ἐκέλευον in the historians where no idea of duration can have been in mind."[2]

[1] *Op. cit.*, p. 92.   [2] *Op. cit.*, p. 17.

The results of Hultsch's study[1] furnish further evidence
that the passages cited from John contain nothing un-
Greek. He found in Polybius that when verbs were
joined by καί the transition from aorist to imperfect was
more common than the reverse; and he cites examples of
this transition not only with λέγω but also with other
verbs of saying. His examples of verbs whose imperfect
is joined with καί to a preceding aorist fill four pages
(pp. 25–28); while aside from other connectives, those
joined by μέν . . . . δέ . . . . fill five pages (pp. 30–34).

It is not, therefore, surprising to find in Epictetus and
the papyri an aorist followed by an imperfect; e.g.,
Epictetus iv. 1. 73: "And who told (aorist) you that walk-
ing was an action of your own that cannot be restrained?
For I only said (imperfect) that your exerting yourself
toward it could not be restrained." Compare ii. 16. 16,
and P. Oxy. VI, 930 (letter, ii/iii A.D.), lines 11 f. John's
use of this sequence cannot, therefore, be regarded as
un-Greek.

5. COGNATE DATIVE

Montgomery (p. 16) mentions with other "Semitic constructions" John 3:29, χαρᾷ χαίρει, in which he finds the
infinitive absolute represented.

There can be no doubt that this construction was used
in the Septuagint to translate the infinitive absolute;
Thackeray estimates its occurrence there at about 200
times. And Walter Bauer (*Wörterbuch*) feels sure that its
use in John is due to the influence of this Old Testament

---

[1] *Die erzählenden Zeitformen bei Polybius* (Leipzig, 1891–93), Vol. III.

usage. He refers to Isa. 66:10, where this exact phrase occurs.

But it is interesting to note that Thackeray still concludes that it existed as a good Greek construction in the Koine. Moulton's argument[1] against Blass has been carried further by Radermacher,[2] who emphasizes the importance of the many parallels in Attic Tragedy and Old Comedy, and concludes that "only the wide extension of this construction in the New Testament is to be regarded as Semitic." Howard (p. 443) and Burrows (p. 103) quote Radermacher's conclusion with approval.

Several idioms that appear in the papyri resemble this but are not exactly identical; for example, the common formula: P. Lond. II, 262 (sale of a house, 11 A.D.), line 6: βεβαιωσω παση βεβαιωσει επι τον απαντα χρονον. A very close parallel occurs at the end of the salutation in a later Christian papyrus: P. Oxy. VIII, 1162 (letter of a Christian priest, iv A.D.), line 5: χαρᾷ χα[ί]ρειν. This may be an imitation of John, as John's use is of the Septuagint.

The assumption that the solitary instance in John in which a cognate dative is found is due to translation from a Semitic original runs contrary to the grammarians' opinions quoted above and also to Dalman's statement that this construction was, apart from the Targums, quite unknown "in the Palestinian Aramaic of the Jews."[3]

---

[1] Cf. *A Grammar of New Testament Greek, I. Prolegomena*[3] (Edinburgh, 1908), p. 75.

[2] *Op. cit.*, p. 129. Cf. Kühner-Gerth, *op. cit.*, § 410, 2, Anmerk. 4.

[3] *Words of Jesus*, p. 34.

6. "Go and Do" for "Continue To Do"

Montgomery (pp. 16–17) cites John 15:16, *ἵνα ὑμεῖς ὑπάγητε καὶ καρπὸν φέρητε*, as representing the Hebrew and Aramaic *halak*, "which is used commonly in the sense 'to go on doing.'"

No passage in the papyri or Epictetus was found which could be translated as Montgomery translates John 15:16, "that *you should go on* bearing fruit." Nor does it seem necessary to translate the verse in that fashion. It is much more logical to regard this as the command which Jesus gave his disciples when he chose them.

What we have, then, in this clause is Jesus' orders phrased indirectly. And Burrows (p. 118) offers a different Semitic background which is based on this understanding of the passage:

The expression "go do something" (especially in the imperative and generally without a conjunction) is characteristic of Aramaic and Syriac; e.g., Ezra 5:15. . . . . This idiom doubtless underlies the *πορευθείς* of the Synoptics and may account for the *ὑπάγητε* in John 15:16.

However, this usage is common in Greek in the imperative with or without the conjunction. Thus this use of "Go" as a rather superfluous introduction to an order is quite frequent in Epictetus; e.g., iii. 22. 5: "Go [*ὕπαγε*]; make your circuit, and thus intimately move everything. . . . ." Compare also iii. 21. 6; 23. 12; etc. Ἀπέρχομαι is used frequently by Epictetus in the same way; so in i. 4. 15: *ἄπελθε καὶ μὴ μόνον ἐξηγοῦ τὰ βιβλία, ἀλλὰ καὶ γράφε αὐτὸς τοιαῦτα.* Compare i. 2. 16; 24. 5; iv. 11. 34; etc. Thus John 15:16 is well attested in contemporary Greek usage.

7. PRONOUN, COPULA, PREDICATE

In commenting on John 15:1, ἐγώ εἰμι ἡ ἄμπελος, Montgomery (p. 18) remarks, "The use of both pronoun and predicate verb is hardly Greek, which would generally find one or the other term sufficient." He explains the construction as the laborious spelling-out of the Aramaic *ena hu gefitta* by three words, the *hu* ("it") being rendered by the copula.

It is true that in Greek it is possible to omit the predicate verb in such a sentence. But the occurrence of subject pronoun, copula, and predicate nominative is common enough in Hellenistic Greek to make the hypothesis of a singularly slavish mistranslation of an Aramaic idiom unnecessary. In addition to the examples[1] of this construction which have been quoted from inscriptions, magical papyri, Hermetic and Mandaean literature, and later Christian literature, the following may be noted: Plutarch *Moralia* (ed. Bern., pp. 478–79) quotes an inscription in honor of Isis: ἐγώ εἰμι πᾶν τὸ γεγονὸς καὶ ὂν καὶ ἐσόμενον. In the magical papyrus Bib. Nat. suppl. gr. 574 (iv A.D.) the construction is frequent. σὺ εἶ plus a predicate nominative occurs 9 times in succession in lines 2982 f. In line 3269, the speaker is to supply his name: "I am So-and-So." Elsewhere this construction is found in lines 185 f., 385, 1018, 1075, 1190, 1177, 1498, 1644, 1637, 1936, 2211, 2198, 2999, and 3107.

[1] Cf. Deissmann, *Bible Studies* (Edinburgh, 1901), p. 355; *idem, Light from the Ancient East* (4th ed.; London, 1927), pp. 138 ff.; J. H. Moulton and G. Milligan, *The Vocabulary of the Greek Testament* (London, 1929), *s.v.;* W. Bauer, *Das Johannesevangelium*[2] (Tübingen, 1925), Excursus to 8:12.

The impression gathered from a study of all these instances is likely to be that this idiom occurs only in reli-
gious liturgy, the literature of obscure oriental sects, and
the magician's strange lore. Over against this should be
set its use in Epictetus, where it occurs in every sort of
emphatic declaration of identity. The teacher uses it to
declare to a man his true nature: ii. 8. 11: σὺ ἀπόσπασμα
εἶ τοῦ θεοῦ· . . . . ii. 17. 33: σὺ θεὸς εἶ, ὦ ἄνθρωπε, ...
He uses it to state his own relationship to his disciples:
ii. 19. 29: Καὶ νῦν ἐγὼ μὲν παιδευτής εἰμι ὑμέτερος, ...
It is used in an imaginary dialogue: iii. 1. 23: 'ἐγώ εἰμι
τοιοῦτον οἷον ἐν ἱματίῳ πορφύρα.' The tyrant uses it for his
boast: i. 19. 2: 'ἐγώ εἰμι ὁ πάντων κράτιστος.' The citizen
to declare his trade: iv. 8. 16: 'ἐγὼ μουσικός εἰμι' ... 'ἐγὼ
χαλκεύς εἰμι.' The student to deny his bondage: iv. 1. 8:
'πῶς γάρ', φησίν, 'ἐγὼ δοῦλός εἰμι; . . . . . With these last
two passages, compare: BGU II, 511 (record of a trial
before Claudius), col. III, line 9: ['Εγ]ὼ μὲν οὔκ εἰμι
δοῦλος οὐδὲ μουσικῆς [κεν]ός· . . . . . BGU IV, 1079 (letter,
41 A.D.), lines 13 f.: ἐγὼ παιδάριν εἰμι· . . . . . Compare
also Epictetus i. 10. 6, 7; 27. 17; iii. 22. 5, 6, 88; iv. 7. 31;
8. 15, 25, 26; 13. 11. The evidence of Epictetus alone is
sufficient to show that John's use of this construction is
very possible Greek indeed.

8. Ὄνομα αὐτῷ FOR "HIS NAME"

This construction, which occurs in John 1:6 and 3:1,
is regarded by both Montgomery and Burney as due to
Semitic influence. Most of the Semitic parallels cited do
not seem very convincing. Why should the dative have a

parallel in Ezra 5:14, "Sheshbazzar his name," as Montgomery (p. 16) suggests? Would not ὄνομα αὐτοῦ be a
closer parallel to the Semitic construction? And what
consideration is due the long list of parallels from Syriac
given by Burney (pp. 30 f.) in almost all of which there is
a relative pronoun? The only significant item in the evidence adduced is the Septuagint use of this construction
to render the Hebrew שמו . But the translators used this
form, as they did the genitive, because it was a current
Greek way of saying "his name."

The significance of the fact "that the only other occurrences of ὄνομα αὐτῷ are found in the Apocalypse, which
is strongly Semitic in colouring"[1] is somewhat dimmed by
the occurrence of the phrase in the following: Xenophon
Anabasis i. 5, 4: ἐνταῦθα ἦν πόλις μεγάλη, ὄνομα δ' αὐτῇ
Κορσωτή;[2] Herodotus 1. 179: ἔστι δὲ ἄλλη πόλις . . . . Ἴς
ὄνομα αὐτῇ;[3] Aelian *Nat. an.* 8, 2: γυνὴ . . . . Ἡρακληὶς
ὄνομα αὐτῇ.[4]

Compare also the following passages from Plutarch:
De Iside et Osiride (ed. Bern., pp. 484–85): ὅπου τῇ πόλει
μέχρι νῦν ὄνομα Κοπτώ ; ibid. (p. 486): ὄνομα δὲ τῷ μὲν
βασιλεῖ Μάλκανδρον εἶναί φασιν· αὐτῇ δ' οἱ μὲν Ἀστάρτην
οἱ δὲ Σαῶσιν. . . . .

Nor is this construction entirely unknown to the *Dis-*

---

[1] Burney, *op. cit.*

[2] Quoted with similar examples by Kühner-Gerth, *op. cit.*, § 356, 2.

[3] Quoted with other examples by Pallis, *Notes on St. John and the Apocalypse* (Oxford, without date), p. 1.

[4] Quoted with other examples by Walter Bauer, *Griechisch-deutsches Wörterbuch z. d. Schriften d. Neuen Testaments* (Giessen, 1928).

courses and the papyri. It occurs three times at least in
the following papyrus: P. Oxy. III, 465 (astrological calendar, ii A.D.), col. I, line 12: ὄνομα αὐτῷ ἐστιν Νεβύ, and
col. V, line 159; col. VII, line 199. It occurs in the magical
papyrus Bib. Nat. suppl. gr. 514 (iv A.D.), in the form
ὄνομά σοι, 12 times in lines 1637–95, and frequently elsewhere. It is found twice in the *Discourses* in the form of
an indirect question: ii. 10. 12: 'ἐπελάθου, τίς εἶ καὶ τί
σοι ὄνομα'; iv. 12. 16: τίνες ἐσμὲν καὶ τί ἡμῖν ὄνομα, ...

These examples show that what is needed to complete
the Johannine expression is not a relative pronoun, as
Burney argued, but the verb "to be." And the proof of
this lies in John 18:10: ἦν δὲ ὄνομα τῷ δούλῳ Μάλχος. The
supposition that ὄνομα αὐτῷ is a Semitic construction in
John is possible only if New Testament Greek is regarded
as an isolated language; it is obvious, as Burrows (p. 101)
admits, that it is Greek.

9. PLURAL VERB WITH SINGULAR SUBJECT

Montgomery (p. 16) mentions this as a Semitic construction and claims John 7:49, "This multitude which
knows not the Law are accursed," as an example of it.
More exactly, however, what we have here is a collective
subject with a plural verb from which it is separated by a
participial clause. Burrows admits (p. 115) that "this is
not especially significant: a plural verb with a collective
noun is not unnatural in any language." Yet he classifies
it with Aramaisms in John which may be due to the author's thinking in Aramaic while writing in Greek!

In classical Greek such a construction would pass with-

out comment. Gildersleeve remarks[1] that "nouns of multitude often take the verb in the plural," and (among
others) gives the following examples: Xenophon *Hell.*
iii. 3. 4; Plato *Laws* 948C; Aeschylus *Ag.* 189; Pindar
P. ii. 46–47; Homer *Iliad* ii. 278. That the construction
persisted through Hellenistic times is shown by a similar
use in P. Fay. 117 (letter, 108 A.D.), lines 24 f.: [κα]ὶ
γράφις μυ λεί⟨α⟩ν ὅτι εὐχαρι[σ]τῶ τῇ κόμῃ ὥτε τέσσαρες
[στ]α[τ]ῆρας καθ᾽ ὑμῶν γεγραφήκασι. Adequate instances
of this usage in later Greek are given by Jannaris.[2]

10. CASUS PENDENS

This "Semitic" construction is found in 27 passages
which Burney (pp. 63 f.) quotes from John: 1:12; 3:26;
etc. The examples he gives may be grouped in three
classes according as the pronoun follows and "picks up"
(1) a relative pronoun (e.g., 3:32), or (2) a participle used
as a substantive (e.g., 1:33), or (3) a noun (e.g., 1:18).[3]
This construction occurs in John 12 times with the relative pronoun, 10 times with the participle, 5 times with a
noun.

The nominative of the participle or noun in this "absolute" construction was fairly frequent in classical
Greek. Walter Bauer speaks of ἐκεῖνος after a participial
subject as "abounding."[4] Winer-Moulton (p. 718) men-

---

[1] *Op. cit.*, p. 54.   [2] *Op. cit.*, § 1174.

[3] It is to be noted that this construction with the relative pronoun is
not the same as the relative completed by a pronoun. In that case the
pronoun occurs in the relative clause; in this case, in the following clause.
Noteworthy also is the fact that in the third class the noun, always a
nominative, is followed by a relative or participial clause.

[4] *Wörterbuch, s.v., ἐκεῖνος.*

tions it with some particular kinds of anacolouthon which have especially established themselves in Greek usage, and cites Xen. *Cyr.* ii. 3. 5, *Ec.* 1. 14, *Ael.* 7. 1. Gildersleeve quotes from Plato, Isocrates, Andocides, Xenophon, Herodotus, Euripides, Aeschylus, and Homer.[1]

Many of the references already given treat also of the *casus pendens* with the relative pronoun. And Goodwin might have been describing Johannine instead of classical usage in the following:

When a clause containing a relative with omitted antecedent precedes the leading clause, the latter often contains a demonstrative referring back with emphasis to the omitted antecedent; as ἃ ἐβούλετο ταῦτα ἔλαβεν, *what he wanted, that he took*, etc.[2]

Winer-Moulton (p. 186) speaks of this construction as occurring "almost regularly," and cites passages from Xenophon, Plato, and others.

There can be no doubt as to the regularity of this construction in Hellenistic Greek. A fine parallel to the use with the relative occurs in the papyri: BGU I, 19 (lawsuit record, 135 A.D.), col. II, lines 4 f.: Ὅσα προσήναντο πα[τρι?]κῶν περὶ τὸν προκείμενον ἀπὸ τῆς εὐ[δ]αιμονίδος διαθήκης . . . . ταῦτα μετεῖναι τοῖς ἐκείνου τέκνοις. Compare John 1:12, also BGU II, 372 (official decree, 154 A.D.), col. II, lines 19 f., where ἐάν τις occurs in the same construction. The *casus pendens* with the noun in true "Semitic" fashion occurs in BGU II, 523 (letter), lines 21 f.: Τὰς οὖν δραχμὰς ἑξήκοντα δὸς αὐτὰ Ἥλιτι τῷ ἐμῷ.

---

[1] *Op. cit.*, I, 3. Cf. Moulton, *op. cit.*, p. 69; Radermacher, *op. cit.*, pp. 21 f.; Lagrange, *op. cit.*, pp. cx. f.

[2] *A Greek Grammar* (Boston, 1892), p. 210, n. 3.

And in P. Oxy. II, 299 (letter, i A.D.), line 2; P. Oxy. II, 268 (repayment of a dowry, 58 A.D.), line 2. The same construction, but with the participle, also occurs in the papyri, e.g., P. Fay. 127 (letter, ii/iii A.D.), line 5: καλῶς ποιήσις τῷ ἐπιβάλλον ὑμῖν τοῦ καρποῦ τοῦ ἀμπελῶνος δ[ο]ῦναι αὐτό. . . . . Compare BGU II, 385 (letter, ii/iii A.D.), line 7.

In Epictetus the construction occurs so frequently as to make an adequate presentation of his use difficult. The participle as a nominative absolute occurs in iii. 3. 8: καὶ λοιπὸν ὁ τῶν ἐκτός τινων ἐκχωρῶν, οὗτος τοῦ ἀγαθοῦ τυγχάνει. Compare i. 8. 3; 14. 10; 29. 52; ii. 6. 22; 24. 3. That the use with the participle was equivalent to the use with the relative pronoun is shown by ii. 22. 3, where ὅστις . . . . , οὗτος . . . . is co-ordinated with ὁ δὲ μὴ δυνάμενος . . . . οὗτος. . . . .

Of these two equivalent constructions, Epictetus' favorite was the relative completed by a demonstrative, which he uses approximately 75 times with all the forms of the relative pronoun; e.g., i. 25. 2: περὶ ἃ ἐσπουδάκαμεν, τούτων ἐξουσίαν οὐδεὶς ἔχει· ὧν ἐξουσίαν οἱ ἄλλοι ἔχουσιν, τούτων οὐκ ἐπιστρεφόμεθα. Compare i. 9. 21; 24. 13; 25. 24; 27. 2; 29. 64; ii. 1. 24; 2. 21; 5. 12, 21; 7. 11; 10. 23; 12. 11; 13. 14; 16. 37; 21. 4, 17, 18; 22. 1; 23. 39; iii. 1. 4, 44; iv. 1. 77, 99; 6. 5; 10. 14; 3. 3.[1]

But Epictetus does not completely slight the form of the construction in which a noun is completed by a personal or demonstrative pronoun, although, like John, he

[1] For further examples, cf. Schenkl's Index, *Epicteti Dissertationes ab Arriano Digestae, Editio Maior.*

uses it infrequently; e.g., iv. 5. 28: ἀλλὰ τὸ περὶ ἑκάστου
τούτων δόγμα, τοῦτό ἐστι τὸ βλάπτον, ... Compare i. 6.
9, 32; iii. 1. 22; iv. 6. 16.

Moreover, Epictetus uses οὗτος after εἴ τις, ἐάν, ὅταν,
ἐπειδή, ὅτι, ὅπως, and numerous other conjunctions in a
lavish fashion that far surpasses John.[1] He shares with
John a very similar idiom that is often regarded as Semitic: ὅπου . . . . ἐκεῖ. Compare iv. 4. 15; 11. 25; 7. 14, 36,
and often.

The wide range of the *casus pendens* in classical and
Hellenistic Greek and, especially in Epictetus, renders
the assumption of an Aramaic original as the explanation
of occurrences in John unnecessary.

11. A Term Indicating Place after a
Geographical Name

This "distinctively Aramaic" idiom which indicates
that the place named is a city, country, village, place,
etc., is recognized by Montgomery (pp. 14 f.) in four
Johannine passages: 11:54; 7:42; 19:17; and 11:1. And
Burrows (p. 117) classifies these with Aramaisms which
may be due to thinking in Aramaic.

These four passages furnish us with examples of two
Greek idioms: John 11:54 and 19:17, the use of λεγόμενος
with the term indicating place before or after a geographical name; John 7:42 and 11:1, a geographical name followed by a term indicating place. It is, perhaps, significant that in the latter case, where λεγόμενος does not
occur, there is an additional phrase defining the κώμης.

[1] Cf. Schenkl's Index, *s.v. οὗτος.*

The Johannine construction with λεγόμενος is very common in the papyri. The frequency of the idiom and the variety of places so indicated is shown in the following examples, where in each example a different type of place, such as village, alley, square, etc., is mentioned: P. Oxy. I, 99 (sale of house, 55 A.D.), line 7: εἰς τὴν τῶν ποιμένων λεγομένη⟨ν⟩ λαύρα⟨ν⟩ ; P. Oxy. II, 249 (registration of property, 80 A.D.), line 15: ἐν τῷ Παμμένους λεγομένῳ παραδείσου [= παραδείσῳ]; P. Teb. II, 311 (lease of land, 134 A.D.), lines 17 f.: ἐν τῷ λεγωμένῳ Νεοφύτῳ γύῳ; P. Oxy. VI, 918 (land survey, ii A.D.), col. II, line 13: λιβὸ(s) Τεκνάνις λεγομ(ένη) διῶρυξ . . . . ; BGU I, 217 (receipt, ii/iii A.D.), line 4: ἐν τόπῳ Πκαλσινα λε[γ]ομένο[υ] . . . . . For further examples, cf. P. Lond. II, 358 (petition, ca. 150 A.D.), line 4; P. Lond. II, 289 (ratification of sale, 91 A.D.), line 14; P. Teb. II, 382 (division of land, 30 B.C.—1 A.D.), col. II, line 6; BGU I, 139 (declaration of property, 201 A.D.), line 9; P. Oxy. II, 254 (census return, ca. 20 A.D.), line 3; and others.

The second form of the construction, that which lacks λεγόμενος, is as common to Greek usage as the one just discussed. Gildersleeve quotes Herodotus 2:59: ἐς βού-βαστιν πόλιν . . . . βούσιριν πόλιν . . . . , and many similar examples.[1] Kühner-Gerth (§ 462, a) quotes passages from Thucydides and Herodotus in which islands, cities, mountains, etc., are designated in the same way. The same constructions are found in Plutarch's *Greek Questions;* e.g., 293A (ed. Halliday, p. 19): Κέρκυραν τὴν νῆσον; and 298A (p. 27): Σάνην μὲν πόλιν.

[1] *Op. cit.*, II, 245.

The frequent recurrence of πόλις, κώμη, κλῆρος, μέρος, κτλ., in the papyri will, with Plutarch's help, make up for the lack of this construction in Epictetus. The formulas in which the names of the leading cities occur (e.g., απο κωμης Σοκνοπαιου Νησου) are found again and again. And the names of less important cities and villages occur in the same construction: P. Oxy. III, 488 (petition, ii/iii A.D.), line 11: ἐν κλήρῳ λεγο(μένῳ) Διαγραφῆς ἐν πεδίοις Κρήκεως κώμης. . . . . Compare P. Oxy. III, 485 (notification to the strategus, 178 A.D.), line 15; P. Fay. 120 (letter, 100 A.D.), line 6; P. Oxy. I, 39 (release from military service, 52 A.D.), line 10; P. Oxy. IX, 1185 (letter of a prefect, ca. 200 A.D.), line 27; BGU I, 112 (declaration of property, 58–59 A.D.), line 2; P. Oxy. II, 270 (indemnification of a surety, 94 A.D.), line 22; and many others.

12. Puns in John

Montgomery (p. 16) calls attention to the play on τὸ πνεῦμα which is used to mean "wind" and "spirit" in John 3:8. Burrows, who lists this (p. 117) with Aramaisms which may be due to thinking in Aramaic, claims that, though possible in Greek, it "would more readily occur to a Semitic mind."

It is true, as Bernard says,[1] that "elsewhere in the New Testament πνεῦμα never has its primitive meaning 'wind' "; but by "primitive meaning" Bernard here means "Greek meaning," and *pneuma* very clearly has this meaning of "wind" in classical and Hellenistic Greek. The classic study of this word by President Burton[2]

---

[1] *St. John*, pp. 106–7.

[2] *Spirit, Soul, and Flesh* (Chicago, 1918), p. 13.

states that it occurs with the meaning "wind" in Aeschylus, Sophocles, Euripides, Aristophanes, Herodotus, Thucydides, Demosthenes, Plato, and Aristotle, and gives examples of this usage. The only possible difficulty, then, would be whether the author of the Fourth Gospel would, as a Greek, know the meaning "spirit" for *pneuma*. The results of the study mentioned above indicate that in Greek usage *pneuma* had come to have a distinctly vital sense as in the writings of Aristotle and Epictetus, but no such meaning as in Old Testament and Christian usage. The author of the Fourth Gospel was, however, a Christian; and in such circumstances it is hard to see what argument as to Semitic origins can be based on this word-play.

Walter Bauer, in commenting on John 2:22, notes more than 25 instances in which the Greek words in the gospel are given a double meaning. Several of these are possible only in the Greek. For example, Field, in commenting on ἄνωθεν in John 3:3,[1] seems reluctant to accept "again" in spite of Artemid. *Onirocr.* 1. 13, which he quotes, because no example of this use of the word is found in John, and because "the Hebrew equivalent is always *local*." In other words, the double meaning is possible in Greek but not in Semitic usage. The best evidence for the double meaning in John is found in the fact that in the *Discourses* ἄνωθεν is used in both senses. It occurs in i. 30. 1 with the meaning "from above," and in the following passage it plainly means "again": ii. 17.

[1] *Notes on the Translation of the New Testament* (Cambridge, 1899), pp. 86 f. Cf. Abbott, *Johannine Grammar* (London, 1906), § 1907, where the same statement is made for Aramaic.

27: οὐ θέλεις ἀπομαθεῖν, εἰ δυνατόν, πάντα ταῦτα καὶ ἄνωθεν ἄρξασθαι. . . . . Olsson insists on the latter meaning in his note on BGU 595, lines 6–7: ἀποδέδωκε αὐτὰς ἄνωθον [= ἄνωθεν].[1]

All this indicates that word-play in John favors a Greek rather than a Semitic original.

13. "Living Water"

This phrase, which occurs in John 4:10, 11, and 7:38, is Semitic, so Montgomery claims (p. 16); and he points out that Rev. 7:17 is the only other occurrence in the New Testament. And Burrows (p. 117) lists it as possible evidence that the author was thinking in Aramaic.

That the phrase does not demand an origin in Aramaic is shown by its occurrence in the Didache (vii. 1, 2): βαπτίσατε εἰς τὸ ὄνομα . . . . ἐν ὕδατι ζῶντι. ἐὰν δὲ μὴ ἔχῃς ὕδωρ ζῶν, ... The phrase was common in the Septuagint, e.g., of God as πηγὴ ζωῆς Ps. 35:10, etc.; and Bernard[2] cites Cant. 4:15, "where the mystic bride is described as φρέαρ ὕδατος ζῶντος." A possible explanation of this phrase in John is, therefore, the influence of Septuagint phraseology.

But the most probable explanation is that the use of

[1] *Papyrusbriefe aus der frühesten Römerzeit* (Uppsala, 1925), p. 135.

[2] *Op. cit.*, pp. 138–39. Walter Bauer (*Das Johannesevangelium*, Excursus to 4:14) claims that "living water" had a long history, especially in the Orient, and goes back to the ancient Babylonians. He believes that the gnostic books quoted by Hippolytus (*Elench.* v. 19. 21; 27. 2) are independent of John when they speak of τὸ ποτήριον ζῶντος ὕδατος ἀλλομένου and τοῦ ζῶντος ὕδατος . . . . πηγὴ ζῶντος ὕδατος ἀλλομένου. But Wendland (*Hippolytus Werke*, Vol. III, *loc. cit.*) sees Johannine influence here.

"living" in the phrase ὁ θεὸς ὁ ζῶν (*the true God*, or *the real God*) influenced this phrase in John as well as others. For in John, Jesus is not only "living water," he is also (6: 51) ὁ ἄρτος ὁ ζῶν. The close association of the idea of "heavenly" with this "living bread" in chapter 6 bears out the suggestion that it is from the association of Jesus with the "living God," the "God of Heaven," that these titles of "living bread" and "living water" came to be given to him. In any case, whatever explains "living water" must also explain "living bread," and an Aramaic original will hardly do that.

CHAPTER III

THE PARTS OF SPEECH

1. PRONOUNS

a) RELATIVE PRONOUNS

Burney[1] finds the Semitic use of the indeclinable relative pronoun completed by a pronoun in seven passages in John: 1:6 (cf. 3:1); 1:27; 1:33; 9:36; 13:26; 18:9.

Not one of these corresponds to Burney's example, "I saw the man who I gave the book to him." The assumption that 1:6 and 3:1 omit a relative is untenable, as the Greek parallels quoted on pages 35 and 36 will show. In 9:36 Burney assumes that ἵνα is a mistranslation of the relative ד. In 1:33 the Semitic construction would be much plainer if there were but one participle. It may be noted also that 1:27 closely resembles the parallel in Mark 1:7. This is the only one that Burrows regards as a fine example of the Semitic construction, and this in his words[2] "proves nothing here, because John may have quoted it from the Synoptics." Driver[3] thinks that 18:9 was included here by Burney "by an error as it does not come under this category at all," and "the Greek is perfectly correct" being exactly paralleled in Xen. *Cyrop*. VI. iv. 9. And in 13:26 the compound predicate should not be overlooked. The plain Semitic flavor of such a transla-

---

[1] *The Aramaic Origin of the Fourth Gospel*, p. 84.

[2] *The Original Language of the Gospel of John*, p. 106.

[3] *Original Language*.

tion as Gen. 6:17 in the Septuagint, καταφθεῖραι πᾶσαν σάρκα ἐν ᾗ ἐστὶν ἐν αὐτῇ πνεῦμα ζωῆς, is not noticeable in these Johannine passages.[1] Such was Wellhausen's judgment,[2] nor does Bauer cite a single Johannine passage in his list of the occurrences of this idiom in the New Testament.

It is, therefore, with no conviction that John actually has this construction that evidence is adduced to show that even if he did have an occasional instance of it, it would not be un-Greek. Moulton long ago pointed out that this construction had its roots in the classical language.[3] Winer-Moulton[4] cites many passages from classical and Hellenistic authors; and Radermacher quotes Callimachus *Epigr.* xlii. 3; Asclepiodotus *Tact.* 1. 3; and Diodor. i. 97, 2; with the significant observation that this construction is most frequent in writers who stand closest to the popul speech.[5] This evidence supports Driver's contention th t this construction was extended to "single-limbed relati e clauses" in classical Greek.[6]

Further proof of Greek use of the idiom in Hellenistic times is: P. Oxy. I, 117 (letter, ii/iii A.D.), line 14: ῥάκη δύο κατασεσημημμένα [τ]ῇ σφραγεῖδί μου, ἐξ ὧν δώσεις τοῖς παιδίοις σου ἓν ἐξ αὐτῶν. Thackeray regards its presence

---

[1] Lagrange, *S. Jean, loc. cit.*

[2] *Das Evangelium Johannis*, p. 135.

[3] *Prolegomena*, pp. 94–95; cf. Kühner-Gerth, *Ausführliche Grammatik*, § 561, 1, Anm. 2.

[4] *Grammar of New Testament Greek*[9], p. 185.

[5] *Neutestamentliche Grammatik*, p. 217.

[6] Quoted by Howard, *Grammar of New Testament Greek*, II, 435.

in II Macc. 12:37 and I Esdras 3:5, etc., as sufficient
warrant for its existence in the Koine.[1] Further evidence
in this direction is to be found in the fairly frequent use of
this construction in the Septuagint where the Hebrew
does not have it; e.g., Isa. 1:21.[2]

In modern Greek, as in English and German, the idiom
is very much at home, as Moulton pointed out in his *Prolegomena*.[3] The completion of the relative by a pronoun is,
therefore, native enough to the Greek tongue to make an
occasional occurrence of little value as a mark of Semitic
influence. And when these occasional occurrences are as
dubious in character as those cited for John by Burney,
their value is obviously infinitesimal. Moreover, the
presence of the idiom in I Clem. 21:9, οὗ ἡ πνοὴ αὐτοῦ ἐν
ἡμῖν ἐστίν, calls for further caution in drawing conclusions from its occurrence, since here we have a Christian
contemporary of the author of the Fourth Gospel using
this idiom while writing in Greek.

b) Personal Pronouns

(1) "Anticipating a Genitive"

Burney (p. 85) points out that "it is peculiarly idiomatic in Aramaic to anticipate a genitive by use of a
possessive pronominal suffix attached to the antecedent,"
and gives examples from the Aramaic of Daniel and the
Palestinian Syriac of John, chapter 1. He finds but one

---

[1] *Grammar of Old Testament in Greek* (Cambridge, 1909), p. 46.

[2] Cited with this argument by Howard, *op. cit.*

[3] *Loc. cit.* Cf. Pernot, *Revue des études grecques*, XXXVII, 127–29. He
gives evidence for its occurrence in French also. For further examples in
Hellenistic and modern Greek, cf. Jannaris, *Historical Grammar*, § 1439.

instance of this in John, "but this is so striking that it should surely count for much in estimating the theory of translation from Aramaic." The one instance is: John 9:18, τοὺς γονεῖς αὐτοῦ τοῦ ἀναβλέψαντος, which Burney translates, "his parents of him that had received sight."

The significance of the fact that there is but one example of this idiom in John has been well pointed out by Allis.[1] The genitive construction was, as he says, very common in Greek at that time.[2] Hence knowledge of Greek would *not* have acted as a strong enough deterrent to eliminate all the other occurrences of this common Semitic idiom. According to Allis (p. 551), "it occurs 14 times in the Peshitto of John 1, and 16 times in the Palestinian Syriac of the same chapter."[3] The single occurrence in John is due, not to an inability to use a fairly common Semitic idiom, but to ability to use a fairly uncommon Greek idiom.

For, though exact parallels to the Johannine construction can be found in Hellenistic Greek, they are not frequent. In the papyri, parallels occur in P. Oxy. III, 480 (census returns, 132 A.D.), line 2: [οἰ]κ(ίαν) καὶ χρηστ(ήρια) πρότ(ερον) α̣[ὐ(τοῦ)] πατρός μ[ο]υ ; and P. Oxy. III, 498 (contract with stone-cutters, ii A.D.), lines 9 f.: εἰς οἰκίαν

[1] "The Alleged Aramaic Origin of the Fourth Gospel," *Princeton Theological Review*, XXVI, 550 f.

[2] Cf. Jannaris, *op. cit.*, § 1399.

[3] Burrows, *op. cit.*, p. 99, is convinced of the soundness of Allis' objection "that the participial phrase, if a translation, would be a free rendering of an Aramaic relative clause, and that a translator who thus substituted a Greek idiom for the Aramaic clause would not be likely to reproduce so literally the redundant suffix."

σου τῆς ᾿Αντωνίας. Compare P. Oxy. III, 513 (receipt, 184
A.D.), line 24, and P. Teb. II, 374 (lease of crown land,
131 A.D.), lines 15 f. In Epictetus, the nearest parallel
observed was a similar use of the dative case in iv. 1. 134.

These occasional Greek parallels seem a much better explanation of John 9:18 than the very frequent occurrences
of that Aramaic usage cited by Burney.

(2) ANTICIPATING THE DIRECT OBJECT

Burney notes (p. 86) as a "peculiarly Aramaic idiom"
the anticipation of the direct object of a verb by a pronominal suffix, quoting three examples of it from the Palestinian Syriac of John 19:13–34, and claiming 9:13,
῎Αγουσιν αὐτὸν πρὸς τοὺς Φαρισαίους τόν ποτε τυφλόν, as due
to this Aramaic construction. He states that there are no
examples of this construction in biblical Aramaic, and
only a few in Hebrew. Moreover, in none of the examples
he quotes is the pronoun separated from the direct object
it anticipates, as it is in John 9:13.

This construction is very much like that discussed
above. Like it, only one instance is found in John, although this also seems to be a frequent idiom in Syriac;
and the argument of Allis would apply here with practically the same force.

Such a construction was not unknown to classical
Greek. Gildersleeve[1] quotes examples from Homer and
others, and Kühner-Gerth (§ 469, 3) gives numerous examples, several being object of a verb, although in most
of these cases the object precedes the verb. Jannaris

[1] *Greek Syntax*, II, 279.

speaks of this construction as a "rather frequent practice" in the Greek language after 300 A.D.[1]

The existence of the construction in Hellenistic Greek is proved by both the papyri and Epictetus. In the former, such a formula as the following, P. Fay. 106 (petition, 140 A.D.), line 15: ὅθεν ἀξιῶ σαὶ τὸν σω[τῆρα] ἐλεῆσαί με, is fairly common in petitions. Compare P. Lond. II, 177 (petition, 40–41 A.D.), line 23. Similar constructions occur in Epictetus iii. 24. 117; iv. 7. 20; and iii. 1. 12; and P. Oxy. II, 281 (complaint against a husband, 20–50 A.D.), lines 9 f.

When compared with such contemporary Greek usage, the solitary instance in John of this none-too-frequent Greek idiom looks much more Greek than Aramaic.[2]

(3) UNEMPHATIC PERSONAL PRONOUNS OF THE FIRST AND SECOND PERSON

Montgomery[3] regards the "constant use of the personal pronoun" as "due in large part to the Aramaic participial construction which generally required a pronoun." Torrey[4] makes much the same statement, claiming that "this is one of the most striking and certain Aramaisms in John." Wellhausen noted this use in John and saw the confirmation of its unemphatic nature in the fact that αὐτός was combined with these separate personal pro-

[1] *Op. cit.*, § 1401.

[2] Burrows, *op. cit.*, p. 100, has been convinced by Driver and Howard that this usage is good Koine Greek.

[3] *The Origin of the Gospel According to St. John*, p. 19.

[4] "The Aramaic Origin of the Gospel of John," *Harvard Theological Review*, XVI (1923), p. 322.

nouns when emphasis was desired. In his opinion, however, the source of the idiom was the "Vulgärsprache
. . . . in any event not the Aramaic, for it is not (as in
Aramaic) limited to the present."[1] But Burney (pp.
80 f.), who holds the same view as Montgomery and Torrey, argues that the Aramaic use is not limited to the
(present) participle but is found also with perfect or imperfect; and he gives a long list of unemphatic pronouns
of the first and second persons in John which he regards
as due to the translation of the corresponding unemphatic
pronoun in the Aramaic.

The use of separate personal pronouns in John goes
beyond their use in classical Greek. Yet even there, the
use of separate personal pronouns did not always mean
special emphasis. "The emphasis of the first and second
persons is not to be insisted on too much in poetry or fa-
miliar prose. Notice the frequency of $\dot{\epsilon}\gamma\hat{\omega}\delta a$, $\dot{\epsilon}\gamma\hat{\omega}\mu\alpha\iota$. Noteworthy, also, is the return of $\dot{\epsilon}\gamma\dot{\omega}$ in Aeschin. 3."[2] Ebeling
recognizes the unemphatic use in the phrases $\hat{\eta}\nu$ δ' $\dot{\epsilon}\gamma\dot{\omega}$ and
$\ddot{\epsilon}\phi\eta\nu$ $\dot{\epsilon}\gamma\dot{\omega}$ "and in many other cases," quoting as an example *Protag.* 360*d*.[3] Moulton carries this argument on
by asking,

Are we obliged to see a special stress in the pronoun whenever it
denotes the Master, like the Pythagorean $a\dot{v}\tau\dot{o}s$ $\ddot{\epsilon}\phi a$? We may perhaps better describe it as fairly represented to the eye by the
capital in "He." . . . . Generally the pronoun is unmistakably emphatic in nom., from Matthew 1:21 onwards; but occasionally the
force of the emphasis is not obvious.[4]

[1] *Op. cit.*, pp. 141 f.

[2] Gildersleeve, *op. cit.*, I, 35.

[3] *Gildersleeve Studies*, p. 240.

[4] *Op. cit.*, pp. 85 f.

This unemphatic usage, and in particular the use of
the unemphatic "I" of the teacher is quite common in
Epictetus. In the following passage, in which he is argu-
ing for the good intentions of the gods, there is no direct
contrast between him and any other teacher; the amount
of emphasis upon the ἐγώ would have to be weighed in a
very fine scale indeed: i. 1. 8: ἆρά γε ὅτι οὐκ ἤθελον; ἐγὼ
μὲν δοκῶ ὅτι, εἰ ἠδύναντο, κἀκεῖνα ἂν ἡμῖν ἐπέτρεψαν· . . . .
The thing that is stressed is very obviously not the "I"
but the impossibility. So in i. 5. 9–10, the emphasis falls
upon the ταύτην that precedes the ἐγώ. The use of ἐγῷμαι,
claimed as unemphatic by Gildersleeve, is paralleled by
i. 9. 10: Ἐγὼ μὲν οἶμαι, ὅτι . . . . , which begins a new
paragraph, implies no contrast, and serves simply to in-
troduce the important statement of the teacher. The
same thing is true in i. 10. 7 and throughout the *Discourses*. Much more infrequently, ἡμεῖς is used without
appreciable emphasis; e.g., i. 24. 3, where the translators
find no special emphasis. Epictetus has a way also of using σύ of an imaginary opponent without much emphasis
on the pronoun; e.g., i. 4. 13. This Σύ has not appeared before, is an imaginary opponent, and at the end of the
paragraph has become plural. So in i. 12. 31, where σὺ
. . . . ἀποστρέφεις follows a series of verbs without σύ, and
yet no distinction of emphasis is discernible.

If the use of αὐτός in conjunction with the personal pronouns is a proof of their unemphatic nature in John, the
same thing is true of Epictetus. Schenkl lists in his Index
many passages in which αὐτός is used with ἐγώ, σύ, ἡμεῖς,
and ὑμεῖς. In the two following passages from the papyri,

αὐτός reinforces ἐγώ: P. Oxy. II, 294 (letter, 22 A.D.),
lines 13 f.; P. Oxy. II, 298 (letter, i A.D.), col. II, line 54.

The use of the personal pronouns without emphasis is
fairly frequent in the papyri; e.g., P. Oxy. IX, 1216 (letter,
ii/iii A.D.), lines 3 f.: αἰγὼ εὔχομαι . . . . σὺ οἶδάς . . . .
γράφω . . . . σὺ δαὶ οὐκ ἠξίωσάς μαι . . . . ; and P. Oxy. I,
113 (letter, ii A.D.), line 30.

In spite of the use of unemphatic personal pronouns in
Epictetus, John uses the separate pronouns more than
twice as frequently as the Stoic preacher does. Does the
explanation lie in the fact that the wide use of the Aramaic participle led to the use of many more unemphatic
pronouns in John than in Epictetus? Not at all. A careful
survey of the passages in John in which these separate
pronouns occur will convince one that they are almost all
emphatic.[1]

In the number of unemphatic uses, John and Epictetus
are very close together; but Epictetus lacks the sharp
contrasts, the bitter polemic, and the heavy insistence
that loads most of the pronouns in John with emphasis.
The largest numbers of these pronouns occur in chapters
where Jesus is sharply set off from some individual or
group. They are found in thick clusters in his controver-

[1] Lagrange, *op. cit.*, p. cxiv (in speaking of Burney's plea) says, "the
argument is ingenious, but it is very difficult to point out a case where the
pronoun was not intended to have a certain importance: . . . . cf. x. 17.
27. 28 taken by chance from the passages where Burney does not see
special emphasis." Cf. for a similar protest, W. E. Barnes, who reviews
Burney's book in *Journal of Theological Studies*, XXIII (1922), 420, who
adds 18:37 and 19:7 to the "emphatic" list, and feels that "Dr. Burney
lacks caution in his denial of emphasis."

sies with the Jews; they are frequent in Jesus' revelation of his own significance to his disciples; but ἐγώ occurs but once after the eighteenth chapter. In other words, there is no "constant use of the personal pronoun through the book" as Montgomery (p. 19) claims. The distinctive characteristic of John's use of personal pronouns is the extremely large number of emphatic personal pronouns. The example taken at hazard by Montgomery from a saying of John the Baptist, 3:28, "Ye witness that I said (εἶπον ἐγώ), Not am I the Christ," where the ἐγώ is an "apparently superfluous pronoun," is very similar to another declaration of the Baptist, 1:30, ὑπὲρ οὗ ἐγὼ εἶπον, which Blass-Debrunner[1] quotes as an example of emphatic usage of the pronoun. The use of the personal pronoun in John is due to emphasis rather than to Aramaic.

c) DEMONSTRATIVE PRONOUNS

(1) FREQUENCY

Burney's argument (pp. 82 f.) runs as follows: John prefers οὗτος and ἐκεῖνος to αὐτός(-ή), and he uses the former substantively with far greater freedom than do the Synoptists. This "extraordinary fondness" for demonstratives in preference to personal pronouns is due to the close reproduction of an Aramaic original, for Aramaic is richly supplied with demonstrative pronouns.

John's fondness for demonstratives is not to be explained on the basis of his colloquial, "vulgar" style. For in several hundred papyri, the occurrences of these three

---

[1] A. Debrunner, *Friedrich Blass' Grammatik des neutestamentlichen Griechischs* (Göttingen, 1921), § 277, 1.

pronouns are grouped in a proportion closer to that of the
Synoptists than to that of John. The totals are: αὐτός,
69; οὗτος, 49; ἐκεῖνος, 8. Of course, individual papyri do
present more demonstrative than personal pronouns.
But, in general, the evidence of the papyri lends little
support to John's usage.

Epictetus, however, would have seen nothing extraordinary in John's fondness for demonstratives. In a section of his *Discourses* approximately the length of John,
the totals for the three pronouns are as follows: αὐτός, 16;
οὗτος, 76; ἐκεῖνος, 64. When the totals for John—αὐτός,
18; οὗτος, 44; ἐκεῖνος, 51—are set beside these, it is evident at a glance that Epictetus' usage is more "extraordinary" in every case than John's. It does not take a rich
supply of demonstrative pronouns in Aramaic to explain
a Greek usage in John which is so well supported by
Epictetus.

(2) 'Εκεῖνος WITH PERSONAL FORCE

Montgomery (pp. 19 f.) notes the use of the demonstrative ἐκεῖνος in John 19:35. This use, he says, is not
strange to the Aramaist, since the "Aramaic would be
hu yada', which means 'he—*or* that one—is knowing,' the
one pronoun being both personal and demonstrative."
This seems, a priori, more probable than Torrey's conjecture, quoted by Burrows (p. 114), that ἐκεῖνος here
represents the Aramaic גברא ההוא. For, as Burrows
says, a literal rendering of that Aramaic phrase would be
ἐκεῖνος ὁ ἄνθρωπος.

The use of this pronoun with personal force was not unknown to Greek of the classical period. Kühner-Gerth (§

467, 12) states that it often refers to a preceding substantive or personal pronoun, and that in such cases it indicates no more than the third person.[1]

The same substitution is found in Hellenistic Greek, and is quite frequent in the *Discourses* of Epictetus; e.g., i. 29. 18: τίνι προ[σ]σχῶμεν ; σοὶ ἢ αὐτῷ; καὶ τί λέγει ἐκεῖνος ; . . . . . Compare ii. 8. 11; iii. 24. 114; ii. 6. 8. In each of these four passages, Oldfather translates ἐκεῖνος by the pronoun of the third person. The same use appears in the papyri: P. Lond. III, 897, col. II, lines 1–2: λαογραφιας τοτε γαρ ελασσωθεις υπο του προοντος κωμογραμματεως εκ[ε]ινος μεν [τ]οτε εψευσατο.[2] These parallels are sufficient to indicate that in Greek usage ἐκεῖνος might have demonstrative or personal force, and the last furnishes an interesting parallel to John 19: 35.

2. THE VERB

a) λέγω = "SPEAK OF" OR "MEAN"

This is another of those usages which Montgomery (p. 16) calls "Semitic-looking cases"; he finds *amar* so used in Judg. 7:4, and λέγω in John 8:27, "he spake of (ἔλεγεν) the Father to them." The same usage appears in John 6:70.

That this is good classical usage is shown by the discussion of this word in Liddell and Scott, where examples are given from Plato, Herodotus, and others. Attention may be called to a close parallel to John 8:27, which is

---

[1] For examples, cf. also Bauer, *Wörterbuch*, s.v.

[2] Olsson, *Papyrusbriefe aus der frühesten Römerzeit*, p. 144, translates, ". . . . Da lag er. . . . ."

given in another connection by Smyth:[1] Plato *Gorgias*
503C: εἰ ἔστιν, ἣν σὺ πρότερον ἔλεγες ἀρετήν, ἀληθής, which
he translates, "if the virtue of which you were speaking
before is real."

This use of λέγω is as much at home in the writings of
Epictetus as it was in the writings of his predecessors:
ii. 8. 13: δοκεῖς με λέγειν ἀργυροῦν τινα ἢ χρυσοῦν ἔξωθεν;
and ii. 12. 20; iv. 1. 66; in each of these passages Oldfather
translates with "mean" or "speak of." Compare also ii.
8. 4; i. 29. 16; iii. 22. 76; iv. 1. 99; etc. Instances of this
use, though not as frequent as in more literary Greek, also
appear in the papyri.[2]

The construction was obviously Greek usage in good
standing in the days when the Fourth Gospel was written.

b) εἰμί = "There Is"

"The indeclinable *ith*, which denotes abstract existence," equivalent to the English "there is," seems to
Montgomery (p. 19), who is followed by Burrows (p. 115),
to lie behind "the extraordinarily large use of the verb
'to be' in the Gospel."

Such an assumption, however, fails to take into account that the Greek language used εἰμί both as a copula
and to denote abstract existence. Gildersleeve says,
"Strictly speaking the copula is itself a predicate, as is
not unfrequently shown by the translation when it stands
alone or with an adverb,"[3] and he quotes Dem. (58), 16;

[1] *Greek Grammar* (New York, 1916), p. 358.

[2] Cf. Moulton and Milligan, *Vocabulary*, *s.v.* λέγω.

[3] *Op. cit.*, I, 31.

And. 1, 120; Soph. *Ph.* 1241. And Bauer describes one of the uses of εἰμί as equivalent to *es gibt*.[1]

This use of "to be" is quite common in Hellenistic Greek; it frequently occurs in the *Discourses;* e.g., i. 15. 4: 'ἐν πάσῃ περιστάσει τηρήσω τὸ ἡγεμονικὸν κατὰ φύσιν ἔχον.'—Τὸ τίνος;—'Τὸ ἐκείνου, ἐν ᾧ εἰμί'; i. 12. 1: Περὶ θεῶν οἱ μέν τινές εἰσιν οἱ λέγοντες μηδ' εἶναι τὸ θεῖον. Compare i. 22. 15; 12. 5, 6; ii. 20. 23; iii. 24. 102; and P. Oxy. III, 465 (astrological calendar, ii A.D.), col. I, line 21: ἔσται πόλεμος ἀηδία μάχη . . . . ; P. Teb. II, 272 (medical fragment, ii A.D.), lines 3 f.: εν δε [τοι]ς της επιδοσεως χρονοις πλει[σ]ται ⟨αι⟩τιαι της προσφορας εισιν.

It seems reasonable to believe that the Greek use of "to be" both to express abstract existence and as a copula is a better explanation of the frequency of εἰμί in John than is the use of two Aramaic constructions which could be translated by the one Greek verb.

c) IMPERSONAL USE OF A PLURAL VERB
INSTEAD OF A PASSIVE

This construction is mentioned by Montgomery (p. 16) as peculiarly Aramaic, in connection with John 12:16, "When Jesus was glorified, then the disciples remembered that such things were written about him and these things they did to him," i.e., "were done to him." Moulton notes also John 15:6 and 20:2;[2] and Lagrange[3] finds this use only in 15:6.

---

[1] *Wörterbuch, s.v.* εἰμί.

[2] *Op. cit.*, pp. 58–59, so also Burrows.   [3] *Op. cit.*, p. cxii.

There is no doubt that an impersonal plural of verbs of saying was quite common in classical[1] and Hellenistic Greek. But in regard to the use of this construction with verbs other than verbs of saying, which is the case in John, Howard (p. 448) is inclined to admit the Semitic nature of the construction "since this use is uncommon" in Greek. Yet Gildersleeve quotes the following from writers of the classical period:[2] Plato *Laws* 803D, οἴονται . . . . ἡγοῦνται . . . . ; *Republic* 428B, ... βουλεύονται . . . . ; Thucydides vii. 69.2, ... πάσχουσιν . . . . ; Herodotus 2, 106, ... ἔρχονται. . . . . And Moulton[3] follows Lightfoot in quoting the following: Euripides *I T* 1359: κλέπτοντες ἐκ γῆς ξόανα καὶ θυηπόλους.

A fair number of instances occur in Hellenistic Greek: P. Oxy. I. 119 (letter, ii/iii A.D.), line 12: πεπλάνηκαν ἡμῶς [*l.* ἡμῖν] ἐκε[ῖ], τῇ ἡμέρᾳ ιβ ὅτι ἔπλευσες; P. Fay. 117 (letter, 108 A.D.), line 8: πέμσις ἡμῖν εἰς ὗκον ἀτυμαγια καὶ ἐλᾶν, ἐπὶ οὐ ἔχουσι ἐλᾶν νέαν εἰς ὗκον; Epictetus iv. 11. 21: πάλιν περὶ Διογένους ταῦτα γράφουσι; i. 4. 32: ἀλλ' ὅτι μὲν ἄμπελον ἔδωκαν ἢ πυρούς, ἐπιθύομεν τούτου ἔνεκα, ὅτι δὲ τοιοῦτον ἐξήνεγκαν καρπὸν ἐν ἀνθρωπίνῃ διανοίᾳ . . . . δείξειν ἡμῖν ἤμελλον. . . . .

And R. McKenna[4] notes that Pallis has preserved the idiom in each of the passages in John cited above, in his translation of the gospels into modern Greek. He evidently felt nothing foreign to Greek idiom in this construction.

[1] Gildersleeve, *op. cit.*, p. 41.
[2] *Ibid.*, *loc. cit.*
[3] *Op. cit.*, *loc. cit.*
[4] Quoted by Howard, *op. cit.*, p. 448.

d) TENSE

(1) PRESENT FOR FUTURE

This use occurs in John 29 times, according to Burney (pp. 94 f.), who sees in it a translation of the Aramaic present participle used with future force. This is very frequent in Aramaic and the number of occurrences in John seems to him, therefore, to be significant. Twenty-six of the 29 instances occur with the verb ἔρχομαι; e.g., 14:3. The other three instances are 1:29, ... ὁ αἴρων . . . . ; 12:25, ... ἀπολλύει . . . . ; and 17:20, τῶν πισ-τευόντων. . . . .

Several facts should be noted about these examples: First, there is almost complete limitation of this idiom in John to the verb ἔρχομαι; Burney says nothing of any such limitation in Aramaic; in fact, not one of the three examples which he gives contains this verb. Second, the classification of the non-ἔρχομαι passages under this heading depends to some extent upon the interpretation placed upon John's gospel as a whole.[1]

But, aside from these considerations, John's usage would not grate upon the classicist's ear. Burton says of this construction that "it is recognized by all grammarians."[2] Kühner-Gerth (§ 382, 6) remarks that the present of verbs of going, such as ἔρχομαι, πορεύομαι, ... , are not seldom used in a future sense, and cites examples from Homer, Xenophon, and others. Goodwin's description of classical usage might have been written for John: "In

[1] E.g., Burrows, *op. cit.*, p. 115, questions the future force of αἴρων in 1:29.

[2] *Op. cit.*, pp. 9–10.

animated language the present often refers to the future,
to express *likelihood, intention,* or *danger.*"[1] His examples
are from Thucydides and Demosthenes, and he quotes
Lys. xii. 14 for the use of ἀπόλλυμαι with future force.[2]

This usage is fairly common in post-classical Greek.
Twice, Epictetus uses a compound of ἔρχομαι in the present tense as a future, co-ordinating it with a future: i. 25.
18: καπνὸν πεποίηκεν ἐν τῷ οἰκήματι; ἂν μέτριον, μενῶ· ἂν
λίαν πολύν, ἐξέρχομαι. So also in i. 29. 27. But the use of
the vivid present for future is not limited to the verbs of
going in the *Discourses;* e.g., iv. 1. 47, ἀκούεις; iv. 1. 132,
λέγεις; i. 17. 28, εἶ; i. 19. 27, λέγεις. The same thing is true
of the usage of the papyri P. Lond. II, 306 (appointment,
145 A.D.), line 15: ετι δε κα[ι κ]αταχωρει ο Σατορνιλος τα της
ταξεως β[ι]βλια ταις εξ εθους προθεσμιαις, to which passage
the editor adds the note: "Lines 15–16 δε κτλ. *i.e.* Sa-
tornilus shall hand over (present for future as in lines 9
and 11) the accounts of the tax. . . . ." Also, P. Teb. II,
412 (letter, ii A.D.), lines 3–4: καλῶς ποιήσις ἄνελθε εἰς τὴν
μητρόπολιν τοῦ νέου ἔτους ἐπὶ καιγὼ ἀνέρχομε εἰς τὴν πόλιν;
and P. Oxy. III, 528 (letter, ii A.D.), line 24: ἔρχῃ [εἴτε]
οὐκ ἔρχῃ δήλοσόν μυ, which is the appeal of a husband to an
estranged wife, asking about her return. So in P. Oxy. X,
1291 (letter, 30 A.D.), lines 5 f., Olsson translates two presents—γίνεται and ὑπάγει—as futures. Compare P. Oxy.
I, 113 (letter, ii A.D.), line 28, ἐξέρχομαι, and the following
examples from the fourth volume of the Berlin papyri:
BGU IV, 1041 (letter, ii A.D.), lines 15–16; γράψαι εἶ διὰ τὸ

[1] *Moods and Tenses,* p. 11.

[2] Cf. Kühner-Gerth, *op. cit.,* § 382, 5a.

δο[κ]εῖν, ὅτι ἔρχομαί σοι; BGU IV, 1035 (official report, v
A.D.), lines 16–18: Καὶ σὺν θεῷ ἔρχομε μετὰ τὴν αὔριον φέρον
τὸ χρυσικόν.

This evidence which shows that John's usage can be
paralleled from Homer down through Attic and Hellenistic Greek to the beginning of the Byzantine period
makes inevitable an agreement with Lagrange's judgment that this use of the present tense is not to be regarded as a Semitism.[1]

Of the two examples of the participle used in the present tense for the future which were quoted from Burney
on page 61, Montgomery (p. 18) notes only John 17:20,
for which he finds parallels in Acts 2:47 and Dan. 2:13.

Burton describes this use of the present participle as
closely analogous to the use of the present indicative discussed above.[2]

In the papyri this use of the present participle is found
quite frequently. It has been noted by the editor of P.
Lond. II, 306 (appointment, 145 A.D.) in lines 9 and 11.
And Olsson[3] calls attention to the same construction in
P. Strassb. II, 1173, lines 4 f.: [Διὸ] ἐρωτῶ σε καὶ εἰς τὴν
ἐμὴν [καὶ Βάσσο]υ καταλογὴν δοῦναι ὄνους [τοὺς φέρον]τας
τὰ ξύλα, in a note on τοὺς φέροντας: "present for future."
Compare also P. Oxy. II, 245 (registration of cattle, 26
A.D.), line 11; and P. Oxy. II, 244 (transfer of cattle, 23
A.D.), line 9.

"The Hellenistic age," says Radermacher,[4] "loved the
living constructions"; and therefore used a present for a

---

[1] *Op. cit.*, p. cxii.   [3] *Op. cit.*, p. 206.
[2] *Op. cit.*, pp. 58 f.   [4] *Op. cit.*, p. 152.

future more frequently than the classical age of Greek did. The Gospel of John is therefore characterized as a Greek document of the Hellenistic period by its fondness for the use of the present to refer to the future. The parallels that have been cited for the indicative and the participle are sufficient to remove both from any discussion of Aramaisms in John.

(2) FREQUENT HISTORICAL PRESENT TENSE

Burney's argument (pp. 87–90) that this is due to translation of the Aramaic participle runs as follows: The historical present occurs more frequently in Mark and John than in Matthew and Luke. In Mark, 50 per cent of its occurrences are with verbs of saying; in John, 75 per cent. The frequency of the Aramaic participle is shown by its occurrence 99 times in the 199½ Aramaic verses of Daniel; more than half of these are verbs of saying. Theodotion sometimes renders it by a historic present or (more frequently) by an imperfect; in some cases he employs an aorist. Allen[1] and Wellhausen[2] have maintained that the frequent use of the historical present in Mark is due to Aramaic influence. Therefore, concludes Burney, "it can hardly be doubted that in John also the same theory offers an adequate explanation of the same phenomenon."

Montgomery (p. 18) is more cautious in his statement: "How far the constant lively use of the present tense, e.g., at large in chapters 4 and 19, is due to a possibility of

---

[1] *Expositor*, II (1900), 463 ff.; *Expository Times*, XIII (1901–2), 329; *Oxford Studies in the Synoptic Problem* (Oxford, 1911), p. 293.

[2] *Einleitung in die drei ersten Evangelien*[2] (Berlin, 1911), p. 17.

good Greek idiom or how far to the tradition of the equally lively Aramaic participle, I cannot decide."

Montgomery's suspicion that the frequent use of the
historical present might be good Greek idiom is confirmed
by the grammarians' statement of Greek usage: Kühner-
Gerth (§ 382, 2 and 4) claims that it is more frequent in
Greek than in related languages; and Blass-Debrunner (§
321) notes it as common to classic and New Testament
authors. And both these grammars note especially its
occurrence with λέγω and φημί. Thackeray also, taking the
first three books of each of the four leading historians,
finds the historical present in Herodotus 206 times,
Thucydides 218, Xenophon 61, and Polybius 40 times.
And he concludes from these figures, which show a decrease from classical to Hellenistic times, that in the
classical age the historical present was common to the
literary style and to the vernacular, whereas in Hellenistic it was increasingly regarded as vernacular.[1] And
this argument of Thackeray's, quoted by Howard, is
sufficient to convince Burrows (p. 98) that the use of the
historical present in John is no indication of translation.

This change in attitude may explain why the historical
present is so infrequent in Epictetus, but the more probable reason is that there is so little narrative in his *Discourses*. When we find a short narrative, it usually contains historical presents, especially of λέγω and φημί; e.g.,

---

[1] *The Septuagint and Jewish Worship* (London, 1922), pp. 20 f.; for
further examples from classical Greek and for discussion of the manner
of its use there, cf. Goodwin, *Moods and Tenses*, p. 11; Gildersleeve,
op. cit., I, 85-86; Moulton, *op. cit.*, pp. 120-21.

i. 29. 65: καὶ γὰρ Σωκράτης συνεγίγνωσκεν τῷ ἐπὶ τῆς φυ-
λακῆς κλάοντι, ὅτε ἔμελλεν πίνειν τὸ φάρμακον, καὶ λέγει 'ὡς
γενναίως ἡμᾶς ἀποδεδάκρυκεν.' Compare i. 26, 12 and i. 1.
28–30. The small amount of narrative discredits to some
extent the following figures; yet they have a certain significance. From i. 26 to ii. 16, Epictetus uses the various
tenses of λέγω and φημί as follows: present 55 times, imperfect 5, aorist 1, future 4. Not all, nor even a majority,
of these presents are historical; but a fair number of them
are, and the predominance of the present tense is characteristic of Epictetus.

Examples of the historical present can also be garnered
from the papyri. They, however, no more than Epictetus,
furnish a proper hunting-ground for historical presents,
the amount of narrative being relatively slight. But historical presents are found in the narratives of lawsuits,
etc.; e.g., P. Oxy. III, 472 (speech of an advocate, 130
A.D.), col. III, line 46: ἐδεήθη ἡ Διονυσία τῆς μητρὸς . . . .
καὶ ἡ μὲν Ἑρμιόνη δίδωσιν αὐτῇ. . . . . Blass-Debrunner
(§ 321) claims that this construction is frequent in the
papyri. All of this evidence demonstrates beyond the
shadow of a doubt that such use of the historical present
as occurs in the Gospel of John was possible in a document
composed in Greek by a Greek.

The question still remains: How probable is it that the
presence of the historical present in John is due to Aramaic influence? What evidence is available seems to indicate that nothing could be more improbable. The only
objective evidence is to be found in a study of such

"translation Greek" as occurs in the Septuagint and Theodotion's version. The statistics for the Septuagint use of this construction are very interesting: "Out of 337 instances . . . . 232 occur in the four books of Kingdoms, of which 151 are found in I Kingdoms."[1] In other words, the historical present is most frequent in the Septuagint *where there was no Aramaic participle to translate*, in books written in Hebrew. It is obvious, therefore, that neither John nor the author of I Kingdoms is using an Aramaism when he uses this construction.

But, where there is an Aramaic participle in the Old Testament (in the Aramaic chapters of Daniel), did the translators render it by a historical present? No! Allis, in a study (pp. 554 f.) of the translation of "answering and saying" by Theodotion, finds only 4 (out of 30) cases where the participle is rendered by the present, and in each of these the present is preceded by an aorist. Even more impressive is Lagrange's statement: "Out of 99 cases cited by Burney, in which, according to him, the Aramaic [participle] ought to lead to an historical present, Theodotion uses this construction only 6 times."[2]

Since John's use of the historical present can be established as good Greek usage, and since there is evidence against the supposition that the historical present is the equivalent of the Aramaic participle, it seems both unnecessary and inadvisable to invoke Aramaic influence as the explanation of John's use of this construction.

[1] Thackeray, *The Septuagint in Jewish Worship*, *loc. cit.*

[2] *Op. cit.*, p. cxii.

With great care, Burney lists all the imperfects in John.[1] Excessive frequency in the use of the imperfect is supposed to indicate Aramaic influence, as representing the very frequent Aramaic construction of participle plus a substantive verb in description of past events; but John's use is more infrequent than that of Mark and Luke, although above that of Matthew. Burney's explanation is that the small amount of narrative in John gives little occasion for the use of this construction.

The probability that in Greek the imperfect may dispute with the aorist for the right to be regarded as the narrative tense par excellence has been shown by C. W. E. Miller. He gives the following figures:[2]

Author	No. of Imperfects	No. of Aorists	Percentage of Imperfects	Percentage of Aorists
Herodotus, Book vii.......	819	588	58	42
Herodotus, Book viii.......	587	399	60	40
Thucydides, Book vii.......	593	372	61	39
Thucydides, total..........	4,286	3,910	52	48
Xenophon *Anabasis* i–iv....	1,437	880	62	38

His list and discussion include other figures, but only in Polybius, and Arrian's *Anabasis*, Book i, does the aorist predominate.

For non-narrative Greek, the reviewer of Weymouth's article, "On the Rendering into English of the Greek

[1] *Op. cit.*, pp. 90–93. Lagrange's comment, *op. cit.*, p. cxii., is: "Il n'y a rien à en conclure."

[2] "The Imperfect and the Aorist in Greek," *American Journal of Philology*, XVI (1895), 141 f.

Aorist and Perfect,"[1] quotes one of Weymouth's tables
based on "many chapters" of Thucydides and Herodotus.
In it the occurrences of the aorist are 13 in Thucydides,
19 in Herodotus; while the imperfect occurs 8 times in the
former and 4 times in the latter.

In Hellenistic Greek the imperfect occurs at least as
frequently as in John. A rapid count of the imperfects
in Epictetus i. 1–11 gives a total of 70. If this section be
extended to approximately the length of John, the proportionate number of imperfects would be 140. This must
be admitted on Burney's own plea, as approximately
equivalent to John's 167, for there is much less narrative
in the *Discourses* than there is in the Fourth Gospel.
Where narrative is found, however, the imperfect is frequent; e.g., iv. 8. 17–20: διὰ τοῦτο καλῶς Εὐφράτης ἔλεγεν
ὅτι 'ἐπὶ πολὺ ἐπειρώμην . . . . ἦν . . . . ἤδειν . . . . ἐποίουν
. . . . ἐποίουν . . . . ἤσθιον . . . . εἶχον . . . . ἠγωνιζόμην
. . . . ἐκινδύνευον . . . . ἐκινδυνεύετο . . . . ἔβλαπτον . . . .
ἐθαύμαζον . . . . ἐφιλοσόφουν . . . . ἐποίουν. In P. Oxy.
III, 472 (speech of an advocate, 130 A.D.), 55 lines in
length, 10 imperfects occur; in P. Oxy. III, 526 (letter, ii
A.D.), 4 out of 6 verbs are in the imperfect; etc. A note
from the pen of J. H. Moulton[2] gives evidence for wide
variation in Greek usage:

I find that in Milligan's *Selections from the Greek Papyri* there
are 22 impf. to 111 aor.; in Mark 1, 19 impf. to 39 aor.; in Matthew
3 & 4, 7 impf. to 29 aor.; in Polybius (7 pages in Wilamowitz *Lese-
buch*) 37 impf. to 54 aor.; and in Appian (6 pages in *do.*) 90 impf. to

[1] *American Journal of Philology*, XVI (1895), 259.

[2] Moulton and Howard, *Grammar of New Testament Greek*, II, 457.

25 aor. So Appian here uses the imperfect seven times as much as Mark does and Polybius $1\frac{1}{2}$ times.

The existence of Moulton's figures on the proportion of imperfect and aorist in Greek usage suggested a possible value in making such a comparison for John. A rapid count of the aorists in chapters 4–12, where Burney found 118 imperfects, gave a total of 417 aorists in the indicative. This would seem to indicate that in the very area which Burney regarded as most favorable to the use of the imperfect, it was outnumbered by the aorists in the ratio of 4 to 1. This means that in proportion with aorists, John uses fewer imperfects than Herodotus, Thucydides, Xenophon, Polybius, Appian, etc. The closest parallels to John's proportion of imperfects and aorists are found in the figures cited by Weymouth for non-narrative sections in Herodotus (4 imperfects to 19 aorists), and in the figures cited by Moulton from Milligan's *Selections* (22 imperfects to 111 aorists). A count of the aorists in a half-dozen pages of the *Discourses*, and an estimate of the proportionate number in i. 1–11, indicates that the proportion would be about 10 aorists to 7 imperfects, a proportionate use of the imperfect much greater than John's.

For the Greek, therefore, the frequency of the imperfects in John causes no problem. Burney's argument would have been stronger if there had been some Aramaic idiom which would have justified his claiming John's use of the imperfect as infrequent.

Burney found a further (Aramaic) significance in the fact that ἔλεγεν(-ον) occur 46 times in John and 50 in Mark, although they occur but 10 times in Matthew and

23 in Luke. But his claim that "the use of the substantive verb with the participle of *amar*, 'he was saying,' is frequent in Aramaic" is supported by no evidence and weakened by the admission that it does not occur in Daniel. The frequency of this imperfect is not strange to Greek. On the frequency with which it is used where an aorist might be expected in classical Greek, see the statements of Goodwin quoted on page 29. In Epictetus i. 26 —ii. 15, a verb of saying occurs but once in the aorist, 5 times in the imperfect. Both Epictetus and the papyri use this imperfect with aorist force; e.g., Epictetus, iv. 1. 173, and P. Oxy. 1672, lines 16 f.

Burney's argument in regard to this imperfect in particular, as well as to John's use of the imperfect in general, is very unconvincing, and does not establish the probability that John is here reflecting an Aramaic original. Burrows, indeed (p. 98), is convinced that John's use of the imperfect is not an Aramaism.

3. NEGATIVE ADVERBS

a) πᾶς μή = "NONE"

Burney (p. 98) finds this Semitism in John 6:30 and 12:46, and in about a dozen other New Testament passages.

It is interesting to note in this connection Winer-Moulton's judgment (pp. 214–15): "This Hebraism should in strictness be limited to the expression οὐ(μή) . . . . πᾶς, for in sentences with πᾶς . . . . οὐ(μή) there is usually nothing that is alien to Greek usage . . . . ." If the New Testament passages cited by Burney are divided

according to this criterion, the quotations from the Old
Testament will be in a group by themselves; for the former "Hebraistic" usage will be found to occur only in
direct or indirect quotations from the Old Testament,
while the latter "Greek" usage occurs in only one Old
Testament quotation. The Johannine passages go with
the latter group.

Howard (p. 433) quotes the argument of R. Law:

> It seems questionable whether this is a Hebraism as is usually
> said. The explanation of the idiom probably is, not that πᾶς was
> used in a consciously distributive sense, but that, in vernacular
> Greek, the negative was attached in sense to the verb, where we
> attach it to the nominative ('all are not' equals 'none are'). The
> attachment of οὐ to what seems to us the wrong word is not un-
> usual in Greek [e.g. in Aristoph. Vesp. 1091, πάντα μὴ δεδοικέναι=
> μηδὲν δεδοικέναι—J. H. M.] and is invariable in the common οὔ
> φημι τοῦτο εἶναι="I say that this *is not* so.

Radermacher[1] quotes with one or two other examples
Dionysius of Halicarnassus *Ep. ad Pomp.* 756R: οὐκ ἀπὸ
τοῦ βελτίστου πάντα περὶ αὐτῶν γράφων. And Driver (*Original Language*) cites "Aesch. *Prom.* 215: οὐκ ἠξίωσαν οὐδὲ
προσβλέψαι τὸ πᾶν, where οὐ . . . . τὸ πᾶν = 'nothing at all,'"
which Driver regards as a weakening of what was earlier
a very emphatic form. An example from the papyri, cited
by Moulton,[2] is P. Ryl. II, 113, line 12 (133 A.D.), "where
Hieracion of Letopolis, beekeeper, complains of unjust
treatment from persons μὴ ἔχοντας πᾶν πρᾶγμα πρὸς ἐμέ."
Moulton also[3] refers to *CR*, XV, 442; XVIII, 155 where
he quotes a number of examples of πᾶς with prepositions

[1] *Op. cit.*, pp. 219 f.

[2] *Grammar of New Testament Greek*, II, 22, n. 3.   [3] *Ibid.*, I, 245.

and adjectives of negative meaning, and points out the closely allied Koine use of τις with negative.

All of this evidence indicates that the "Semitic" quality of John's usage here is of a very decidedly secondary nature.

b) Οὐκ ἄνθρωπος = "No One"

Burney (p. 98) points out that because the Hebrew and Aramaic word for "man" can be used to mean "anyone," the use of a negative with it makes it equivalent to "no one." He finds "no one" expressed in the same way in John 3:27; 5:7; and 7:46. In a footnote, he claims that ἄνθρωπος = τις is found in John 3:1, 4; 7:23, 51.

Howard (p. 433) refers to the new Liddell and Scott, where under ἀνήρ the following examples are given: VI. 5 *a man, any man* εἴτ᾽ ἄνδρα τῶν αὐτοῦ τι χρὴ προϊέναι; Ar. *Nu.* 1214; οὐ πρέπει νοῦν ἔχοντι ἀνδρί Pl. *Phd.* 114d, etc.; οὐ παντὸς ἀνδρὸς .... ἐσθ᾽ .... 'tis not every one that can go, Nicol. *Com.* 1. 26." But under ἄνθρωπος the only example cited of use equivalent to τις is I Cor. 4:1.

Lagrange, however, says that ἄνθρωπος for "someone," "anyone," is found in Greek, and quotes Aristotle, *Met.* iv, 7.[1] This use of ἄνθρωπος as equivalent to an indefinite pronoun is fairly common in Epictetus; e.g., ii. 13. 1: Ὅταν ἀγωνιῶντα ἴδω ἄνθρωπον, λέγω ...., where the ἄνθρωπον has the same force as the τινὰ in ii. 13. 5: ὅταν ἴδω τινὰ φοβούμενον, as Mrs. Carter shows by her translation: "Whenever I see any one solicitous, I say. . . . ." In i. 19. 17 also, there can be no doubt that it is used in an indefinite sense.

[1] *Op. cit.*, p. cxiii.

The only example of the negative use that was noted was in the title of Epictetus i. 28: Ὅτι οὐ δεῖ χαλεπαίνειν ἀνθρώποις, where the meaning "no one" is indicated by the following i. 28. 10: οὐδενὶ χαλεπανεῖ.

This is not overwhelming evidence that "no man" as the equivalent of "no one" was at home in the Greek language. But it is not absolutely clear that it was at home in the Fourth Gospel. In 3:27, John the Baptist is speaking of himself in contrast to the Divine Jesus; in 7:46, the same contrast between Man and Jesus, the Divine Being, may well have been intended by the author of the gospel; in the second case, the suitableness of "I have not a man to put me in the pool" is plain.

c) οὐ μὴ .... εἰς τὸν αἰῶνα = "NEVER"

Burney (p. 99) regards this idiom in John 4:14, etc., as a translation of the Hebrew and Aramaic idiom "not .... forever." Elsewhere in the New Testament the construction is found only in Matt. 21:19 (Mark 11:14); Mark 3:29; and I Cor. 8:13.

It is hardly possible that Burney regarded the double negative as an integral part of the "Aramaism," since the Aramaic idiom contains but one. As a matter of fact, this double negative with either future indicative or aorist subjunctive was in Hellenistic times a common method of expressing a negative assertion about the future.[1] BGU II, 531 (letter, 70–80 A.D.), col. II, line 18: ὅτι [ο]ὐ [μὴ] με

---

[1] In Ptolemaic papyri, Mayser (*Grammatik*, II, 233) says it is common in the less-cultured papyri, but with the aorist subjunctive only. He gives several examples. See also Olsson, *op. cit.*, p. 133; Blass-Debrunner, § 365; Moulton, *Prolegomena*, pp. 187 f.

λοιπήσῃς. So several times in P. Oxy. I, 119 (letter, ii/iii
A.D.), lines 4, 6, 14, 15. Nor can it be claimed that εἰς τὸν
αἰῶνα is essentially Semitic. Walter Bauer mentions[1] its
use in Greek since Isocrates, and alludes to its use in
P. Oxy. I, 41 (report of a public meeting, iii/iv A.D.), line
11 (cf. lines 2 and 21): Ἄγουστοι κύριοι εἰς τὸν ἐῶνα.

The value of this construction in John as evidence for
an Aramaic original must be estimated in the light of its
use in the Septuagint and in Paul; Burrows (p. 107) follows Driver in regarding it as partly vernacular and partly
due to Septuagint influence.

4. THE ADJECTIVE

a) μέσος AS A NOUN

Wellhausen claimed that in John μέσος was an adjective and not a noun as in Semitic;[2] in regard to this,
Torrey (p. 322) says, "The claim that in John μέσος is an
adjective, not a noun 'as in Semitic,' is refuted by 20:19,
26, εἰς τὸ μέσον." Torrey's position, then, would seem to
be that, in spite of Wellhausen, μέσος is used as a substantive in John and is consequently an evidence of
Semitic origin.

As a matter of fact, both of these positions are half
wrong: μέσος *is* used as a noun in John, but, far from being Semitic, this use is one of the best attested of Greek
constructions at all stages of the development of the
language. In classical usage, "Neuter adjectives and participles are freely employed as substantives in almost any

[1] *Wörterbuch.*

[2] *Das Iohannis Evangelium,* p. 142.

relation . . . . ,"¹ and Gildersleeve supports this statement with examples, including μέσος, from Isocrates,
Plato, Xenophon, Thucydides, and Homer. A glance at
the discussion of μέσος in Liddell and Scott is convincing
proof of the idiomatic nature of its use as a substantive in
classical Greek.²

For the commonness of the construction in the Koine,
no better witness could be found than Epictetus. Like
John, he uses μέσος as a noun in the accusative after εἰς;
e.g., i. 22. 5: κάλει γὰρ αὐτοὺς εἰς τὸ μέσον. The same
phrase occurs in ii. 22. 14, 23, 33; iii. 9. 13; iv. 1. 47; 5. 24.
He also uses μέσος as a noun in the other cases; e.g., with
ἐκ and the genitive in iii. 3. 15, with ἐν and the dative in
iii. 22. 55.

In the papyri, the most common use of μέσος is in the
adverbial expression with ἀνά; e.g., P. Fay. 108 (petition,
171 A.D.), line 10. But the use of the genitive with the
article after ἐκ occurs in BGU II, 388 (lawsuit, ii/iii A.D.),
col. II, line 23. And the persistence of the use in the accusative after εἰς is shown by an instance in a fourth-
century record of some public celebration, P. Oxy. 41,
line 20. Still later use of the adjective as a substantive is
given from the papyri by Moulton and Milligan (*Vocabulary*).

The use of this adjective as a substantive in John,
therefore, is one more instance of this gospel's agreement
with Greek usage.

¹ Gildersleeve, *op. cit.*, I, 13–17.

² For further examples from classical Greek, cf. Winer-Moulton,
op. cit., p. 153; Blass-Debrunner, *op. cit.*, §264, 4; Bauer, *Wörterbuch*,
s.v.; Kühner-Gerth, *op. cit.*, § 462, 1.

b) Superlative for Comparative

Montgomery (p. 16) notes the occurrence of this idiom in John 1:15, πρῶτός μου. Burrows, however, in a study of the Prologue[1] concludes that John 1:15 originated in Greek.

Moulton[2] regarded this as a superlative replacing a comparative; and indeed this use of a superlative where we would expect a comparative is not infrequent in classical Greek.[3] Bernard[4] agrees with Moulton and quotes a similar use of the superlative from Xenophon. Bauer[5] refers to Plutarch *Cato Minor* 18, Sallust *De diis et mundo* 8, p. 257, and Eratosthenes *Catasterism.* c. 42: καὶ πρῶτος ἀνατέλλει καὶ δύνει ἐκείνου.

Abbott,[6] however, took issue with Moulton, claiming that Moulton's main witness, σοῦ πρῶτός εἰμι, from a third-century papyrus, was dependent on John. Moulton's reply[7] was that Abbott, in taking away one witness, had replaced it with two, and thus had established Moulton's position. The examples given by Abbott are taken from scholiasts on Euripides: the first, in the scholiast's Preface to the *Phoenissae:* "Eteocles, as though he were first [in regard] of his brother (ἅτε πρῶτος ὢν τοῦ ἀδελφοῦ)." The second is a scholiast's explanation of *Hecuba* 458, "firstborn palm (πρωτόγονός τε φοῖνιξ)": "created first [in

---

[1] *Journal of Biblical Literature*, XLV (1926), 67.

[2] *Op. cit.*, p. 79.

[3] Winer-Moulton, *op. cit.*, p. 306; Gildersleeve, *op. cit.*, II, 285.

[4] *Op. cit.*, p. 28.

[5] *Das Johannesevangelium*, p. 25.

[6] *Johannine Grammar*, §§ 1896 f., 2666 f.   [7] *Op. cit.*, p. 245.

regard] of the bay-tree (πρῶτον γεννηθέντα τῆς δάφνης)."
Abbott rejected these parallels because of the modern editors' suspicion of such constructions; but Moulton rightly
held that they are valuable parallels for Johannine use.

That confusion of comparative and superlative which
Moulton noticed in illiterate papyri was noted by Sharp[1]
in Epictetus iii. 7. 4. And the use of the superlative where
only two things are compared may be noted in iii. 7. 24.
So also in BGU I, 282 (registration of land, 175 A.D.),
lines 10 f.; P. Oxy. III, 508 (security for a debt, 102 A.D.),
line 5 f.

Here again the hypothesis of Semitic influence is unnecessary; John's construction is Hellenistic Greek.

c) OMISSION OF ARTICLE

Torrey (pp. 323 f.) protests against Wellhausen's claim
that no trace of the construct state is to be found in John,
and finds it in the omission of the article with definite
nouns in John 1:49, 5:29, 5:27, 4:5, 6:68, and 9:5. And
Burrows[2] lists these passages with those that can very
plausibly be explained by the hypothesis of translation.

The omission of the article was common in classical
Greek; e.g., with a predicate noun, after prepositions, or
when the noun modified was completed by a substantive
in the genitive with which it made up a unified phrase.[3]

It may be noted of Torrey's six examples, that three are
predicate nouns, that the phrases in 5:29 also follow a

---

[1] *Epictetus and the New Testament* (London, 1914), pp. 61–62.

[2] "The Original Language of the Gospel of John," *Journal of Biblical
Literature*, p. 124.

[3] Kühner-Gerth, § 461, 1; 462, f, k.

preposition, and that Howard (p. 431) points out the qualitative force of the expression in 6:68 and 9:5.[1]

The following passages, selected from many, indicate that the omission of the article after a preposition was possible in Hellenistic Greek: Epictetus iv. 1. 51: πρὸς εὕρεσιν τῆς ἀληθείας; P. Oxy. IV, 736 (private account, i A.D.), col. II, line 13: μύρου εἰς ἀποστολὴν ταφῆς θυγατρὸς Φνᾶς. Compare P. Oxy. XIV, 1647 (apprenticeship, ii A.D.), line 12.

The article is omitted also where it does not follow a preposition and is used with a noun as definite as those cited by Torrey in John; e.g., Epictetus i. 17. 12: καὶ τίς ἐστιν ὁ γεγραφὼς ὅτι 'ἀρχὴ παιδεύσεως ἡ τῶν ὀνομάτων ἐπί-σκεψις;' P. Oxy. I, 34 (edict, 137 A.D.), col. I, line 17: προσθήσου[σι] δὲ καὶ τῶν κολλημάτων ἀριθμὸν καὶ τὰ ὀνόματα τῶ[ν] συναλλαξάντων. Note in the last passage the variation between the co-ordinate τῶν κολλημάτων ἀριθμόν and τὰ ὀνόματα τῶν συναλλ. The same variation occurs in the *Discourses;* e.g., i. 4. 6: τί ἔργον ἀρετῆς; i. 4. 10: τὸ ἔργον τῆς ἀρετῆς; and also in the following passage, P. Oxy. I, 37 (lawsuit, 49 A.D.), line 19: ἔχω[ι] πρῶτον γράμμα τῆς τροφείτιδος, ἔχωι δεύτερο[ν] τῶν τροφείων τὴν [ἀ]ποχή[ν], where there can be no doubt of the definiteness of either γράμμα or ἀποχήν.

In connection with proper names or definitely known persons, titles often assume the form βασιλεὺς τοῦ Ἰσραήλ; e.g., Epictetus i. 1. 16: σὲ γὰρ οὐκ ἐποίησεν ὁ θεὸς ταμίαν τῶν ἀνέμων, ἀλλὰ τὸν Αἴολον; i. 3. 1: καὶ ὁ θεὸς πατήρ ἐστι τῶν τ' ἀνθρώπων καὶ τῶν θεῶν.

[1] Cf. Moulton, *op. cit.*, p. 83.

The classic study by Völker[1] of the use of the article in the papyri will easily furnish parallels to the Johannine passages cited by Torrey, and a perusal of his brief study will add weight to Bauer's caution that it is hardly possible to make hard and fast rules for the employment of the article.[2] The evidence given here certainly supports Lagrange's conclusion that there is in John no certain example of the construct state.[3]

d) "THE SON OF DESTRUCTION"

This phrase in John 17:12 is regarded by Montgomery (p. 16) as due to the well-known Semitic idiom. The same idiom occurs in 12:36, "sons of light."

Deissmann argues[4] that, though the υἱός of the biblical passages may have been occasioned in the first instance by a Semitic idiom, yet the use of ἔκγονος in the same way by Plato and a similar use of υἱός on inscriptions and coins shows that it is not un-Greek. He makes a distinction[5] in the New Testament occurrences of this idiom between translations on the one hand, and quotations and analogical formations on the other. The instances in the Synoptics he regards as translations. But he regards John 12:36 (cf. I Thess. 5:5) as a quotation, perhaps from Luke 16:8; and John 17:12 (cf. II Thess. 2:3) as an echo of the Septuagint, Isa. 57:4, τέκνα ἀπωλείας.[6]

---

[1] *Syntax der griechischen Papyri. I. Der Artikel* (Münster, 1903).

[2] *Wörterbuch, s.v.*   [4] *Bible Studies*, I, 165–66.

[3] *Op. cit.*, p. cxv.   [5] *Ibid.*, pp. 161 f.

[6] Howard, *op. cit.*, p. 441, is therefore wrong in saying that Deissmann classes John with the Synoptics in the use of this idiom.

It is a striking fact that each of the two instances of this construction in John are paralleled in Paul's letters, and it is possible that the author of the Fourth Gospel may have secured them there. The idiom occurs also in Eph. 2:2; 5:6; Col. 3:6, and Hermas, Vision 3:6:1,[1] as well as in Acts and the Synoptic Gospels.

5. THE NOUN

a) THE PLURAL αἵματα

Montgomery (p. 16) includes this phrase in John 1:13 in a paragraph of "Semitic constructions," and Burrows (p. 116) lists it among Aramaisms which may show that John was thinking in Aramaic.

This position of Burrows' is remarkable when compared with his own statements elsewhere[2] in regard to the re-translation of John 1:13 into Aramaic:

As to the first member of the verse, even if we follow the Greek to the extent of using the plural for the word *blood*, we have only five syllables. . . . . In Hebrew, *blood* is often used in the plural, but I can find no instance in Aramaic. On the other hand, the plural is not at all common in Greek, although it appears occasionally.

Doubt as to the Aramaic nature of this plural was evidently shared by Burney, who "retranslates" the Greek plural by an Aramaic singular; and by McNeille, who claims that the Aramaic plural always means "shed

---

[1] Cited by Bauer, *Wörterbuch, s.v. υἱός.*

[2] "The Johannine Prologue as Aramaic Verse," *Journal of Biblical Literature,* XLV (1926), 66, and n. 22. For Greek usage, cf. Kühner-Gerth, *op. cit.,* § 348, 2.

blood.''[1] Schaeder[2] also uses the singular in his restoration of the original Aramaic of the Prologue, but puts the
plural alongside it in parentheses with a question mark.

On the other hand, that this plural as a Greek plural
presents no problem is shown by the statements of almost
any Greek grammar.[3] And Gildersleeve regards it as so
characteristically Greek, that he uses it in a quotation from
Aeschylus as an example of plural expressions which are
idiomatic in Greek but diverge from English usage.[4] Cadbury[5] in his repudiation of Semitic influence quotes as the
closest parallels in Greek Euripides *Io* 693: ἄλλων τραφεὶς
ἀφ' αἱμάτων; and Plato *Laws*, p. 887D. That this plural,
which Semitic scholars hesitate to recognize as Aramaic,
which Greek scholars claim as Greek usage, can be regarded as evidence of thinking in Aramaic is impossible
on the basis of Burrows' own admission that it is much
more common in Greek than in Aramaic.

b) THE PLURAL ὕδατα

This is classed with αἵματα by Montgomery (p. 16), who
notes that it occurs in Matthew but once and in Revelation several times. Although "water" occurs several times
in John, the plural occurs but once, 3:23.

Much that has been said of the classical use of αἵματα

[1] Referred to by Cadbury (*Expositor*, Vol. II [1924], who finds the
meaning of the passage in Greek physiology.

[2] Reitzenstein-Schaeder, *Studien zum Antiken-Synkretismus aus Iran
und Griechenland* (Leipzig, 1926), p. 340.

[3] Winer-Moulton, *op. cit.*, pp. 220–21; Blass-Debrunner, *op. cit.*,
§ 141, 6; Bauer, *Wörterbuch*, *s.v.* αἷμα.

[4] *Greek Syntax*, I, 23–24.   [5] *Op. cit.*

applies here equally well. Kühner-Gerth classifies this
plural with that of "blood" as Montgomery does, but for
a different reason; for the Greek grammarian it is not a
peculiar plural but a common Greek idiom.[1] Mayser
found it in the papyri of the Ptolemaic period,[2] and its
use in Hellenistic times is established by the following
passages: P. Oxy. 1409 (circulars of a strategus, 278
A.D.), lines 18 f.: ἵν[α ε]ὑμαρῶς [τὴν] ἐσομέν[ην τῶν] ὑδάτων
εἴσροιαν, which the editors translate ". . . . the coming
influx of water"; and P. Lond. III, 1177 (accounts of
waterworks commissioners, 113 A.D.), col. I, lines 7–8: των
τεσαρων φροντιστων ι[σ]αγωγη υδατων καστελλων. Compare *ibid.*, lines 10–12, and col. XIV, line 333; P. Oxy. XII,
1427 (order to workmen, iii A.D.), line 4; and Hermas,
Vision 3:2:4; 3:3:5 twice; 3:3:7. In Vision 1:1:3 and
3:2:9, the same body of water is spoken of in the plural
and the singular in the same passage.

Such examples from classical and post-classical Greek
would seem to justify the single plural in John as natural
Greek.

c) THE PLURAL IN εἰς τὰ ὀπίσω

The use of this plural in John 6:66 leads Montgomery
(p. 16) to group this with "Semitic-looking cases"; Burrows (p. 117), however, regards its significance as doubtful.

Its significance becomes still more doubtful when this
phrase and similar phrases are found outside John. Mayser[3] gives half a dozen examples from the Ptolemaic papyri

[1] *Op. cit.*, § 348, 2.
[2] *Op. cit.*, II, 34.   [3] *Op. cit.*, II, 13.

of the use of a neuter plural article with an adverb in a prepositional phrase, and includes ἐκ τῶν ὀπίσω, Petr. ii. 18 (2b). 2 = iii. 23 (246a). Diodorus Siculus (xviii. 27. 1) has a very similar phrase, ἐκ δὲ τῶν ὄπισθεν. A close parallel to the phrase in John occurs in Hermas, Vision 4 : 3 : 7, εἰς τὰ ὀπίσω; and the plural with this adverb appears also in Phil. 3 : 13. When, in addition to all this, its frequent occurrence in the Septuagint is noticed, the probability that John's use is due to Aramaic influence becomes very slight.

6. The Preposition

a) Frequency of περί and Its Confusion with ὑπέρ

This characteristic of John's Greek is noted by Torrey (p. 322), who regards it as due to translation of the Aramaic עַל. Περί occurs in John about 70 times, ὑπέρ about 14 times. Two things are to be noted, therefore, in regard to περί in Greek usage: its frequency, and the possibility of its being confused with ὑπέρ.

The confusion of these two prepositions is noted for classical Greek by Kühner-Gerth (§ 450), which gives as an example of their frequent interchange Demosthenes 6. 35. Jannaris speaks of this interchange as an acknowledged characteristic of the language.[1]

In Hellenistic Greek the same interchangeability has been pointed out by almost every grammarian and lexicographer who has touched this field.[2] In the papyri an

---

[1] *Op. cit.*, § 1686.

[2] Blass-Debrunner, *op. cit.*, § 229, 1; §§ 230 ff. Bauer, *Wörterbuch, s.v.* περί and ὑπέρ for bibliography. Moulton and Milligan, *op. cit., s.v.* περί.

interchange of these prepositions is quite common. Ol-sson[1] lists 4 occurrences of ὑπέρ = περί in his small collection of Papyrus letters of the Roman period. For περί = ὑπέρ, compare P. Oxy. VI, 933 (letter, ii A.D.), lines 6 f.: εὐχόμενος πᾶσι το[ῖς θεο]ῖς πε[ρὶ τ]ῆ[ς σ]ω[τηρίας σου]; P. Teb. II, 408 (letter, 3 A.D.), lines 5 f.: παρακαλῶ σε περὶ υἱῶν μου τῆι φιλοστοργίᾳ τῶν περὶ Σωτήριχον μὴ ἐᾶσαι πυρὸν αὐτοῖς δοθῆναι.

Epictetus plainly shows the equivalence of the two prepositions by using them "in parallel clauses in the same sense":[2] ii. 13. 18: τί οὖν σοὶ μέλει περὶ τῶν ἀλλο-τρίων; .... Τί οὖν ἀγωνιᾷς ὑπὲρ τῶν ἀλλοτρίων; Compare also ii. 13. 11; and for passages in which ὑπέρ is used where περί might be expected: ii. 5. 20; 13. 9. These illustrations of the usage of Epictetus are a most convincing argument for the degree to which these two prepositions were interchanged in Hellenistic Greek.

The "frequent use of περί" in John is not quite as frequent as the use of this preposition in Epictetus and the papyri. But when its frequent use in the *Discourses* in formal and informal headings and the common use with the accusative to designate place in the papyri are taken into account, the frequency is approximately the same. Περί is found 78 times in a section of the *Discourses* equivalent in length to John;[3] and in a proportionate section of

[1] *Op. cit.*, p. 237.

[2] Sharp, *op. cit.*, p. 93; he quotes iv. 1. 82–83.

[3] Mücke, *Zu Arrians und Epiktets Sprachgebrauche* (Nordhausen, 1887), pp. 7 f., gives a total of 388 occurrences of περί in Epictetus, and 82 for ὑπέρ.

the papyri approximately the same number of occurrences is found. Such usage makes it impossible to regard
the frequency of περί or its interchange with ὑπέρ as an
Aramaism in John.

b) ἐκ WITH GENITIVE, USED AS NOMINATIVE

This occurs in John 16:17, "(some) of (ἐκ) his disciples
said . . . . ," which is quoted by Montgomery (p. 17) as
representing "the Semitic partitive use of the preposition
min = 'of.' "

That phrases with ἐκ and ἀπό had largely replaced the
use of the simple partitive genitive in Hellenistic times
was stated by Moulton in his *Prolegomena*.[1] And the use
of a partitive genitive as subject or object of a verb is to
be found in classical Greek, although, as Blass-Debrunner
(§ 164, 2) says, quite rarely. The examples there given
are Xenophon *An*. iii. 5. 16, and *Hell*. iv. 2. 20, where
ἑκατέρων is used as subject of a verb. This usage is common in the Septuagint.

7. THE CONJUNCTION

a) καί ADVERSATIVE

This use of καί as the equivalent of "but" or "and yet"
is claimed by Burney (p. 66) as Semitic, and he finds 26
instances of its use in John.[2]

---

[1] P. 102. Cf. also p. 245: "A full study of prepositions replacing the
simple genitive may be found in Kuhring, *Praepos*., 11 ff., 20. Dr. Rouse
notes that ἀπό is regularly used in partitive sense now: δῶσε μου ἀπὸ τοῦτο,
'give me some of that.' "

[2] Burrows, *op. cit*., p. 112, regards the frequency of this and the two
following usages in John as noteworthy evidence that John was thinking

Kühner-Gerth finds four uses of καί in classical Greek; three of these are attacked by Burney as being Semitic! The adversative use of this conjunction, according to this grammar (§ 521, 4), was common in classical Greek; and this opinion is supported by examples from Thucydides, Euripides, Herodotus, and Plato.[1]

This use of καί is found also in both Epictetus and the papyri; e.g., P. Teb. II, 278 (acrostics, i A.D.), lines 30 f.: ζητῶι καὶ οὐχ εὐρίσκωι, "I seek but do not find it" (editors); Epictetus i. 11. 32: καὶ νῦν ἐν Ῥώμῃ ἀνέρχῃ, ὅτι δοκεῖ σοι· κἂν μεταδόξῃ, οὐκ ἂν ἀπελεύσῃ. Compare i. 5. 4–5; 7. 24; 27. 1; ii. 14. 21; and BGU II, 384 (letter, ii/iii A.D.), lines 7 f.; BGU I, 38 (letter), lines 15 f.

Pernot,[2] in commenting on the adversative force of καί in John 1:10, says, "One would say the same in modern Greek." The idiom would seem, therefore, to have been at home in the language throughout its history; and thus it can be of no value as an evidence of Aramaic influence on John.

b) καί Introducing a Contrasting Incredulous Question

This is the second of the uses of καί in John which were noted by Burney (p. 67) as showing Semitic influence.

Lagrange[3] rejects this opinion, and claims that such a

---

in Aramaic. But the second use occurs only 5 times (and these are included in Burney's total of 26 for the first use), and the third use occurs only 3 times. Moreover, Lagrange, *op. cit.*, p. cvi., limits the adversative use to 1:5 and 17:11. And in comparison with the parallels cited here, John's use is not frequent.

[1] Further examples in Bernard, *op. cit.*, I, 13–14; Bauer, *Wörterbuch.*
[2] *Op. cit.*, p. 127.   [3] *Op. cit.*, p. cvi.

use of καί is very possible in Greek, citing Euripides *Medea* 1398 as an example. Kühner-Gerth (§ 521, 3) also claims it as classical usage, with examples from Euripides, Xenophon, etc.[1]

This use of καί occurs also in Hellenistic Greek; e.g., Epictetus ii. 21. 11: ἄνθρωπ', ἐν οἴκῳ διαπεπύκτευκας τῷ δουλαρίῳ, ... · καὶ ἔρχῃ μοι . . . . καὶ καθήμενος κρίνεις, πῶς ἐξηγησάμην τὴν λέξιν . . . . ; P. Oxy. I, 33 (trial, ii A.D.), col. I, line 7: ἰδὼν Ἡλιόδωρον εἶπεν· Ἡλιόδωρε, ἀπαγομένου μου οὐδὲν λαλεῖς;' Ἡλιόδωρος εἶπεν· 'καὶ τίνι ἔχομεν λαλῆσαι μὴ ἔχον[τ]ες τὸν ἀκούοντα;' Compare Epictetus i. 29. 11; 2. 18; 19. 2. This evidence is sufficient to justify Pernot's verdict:[2] "Again good Greek."

c) καί = "AND SO"

This use, which is "very frequent in Semitic," is found by Burney (p. 68) in John 6:57, 11:48, and 5:10. The infrequency of the construction in John is due, he alleges, to the frequency of οὖν in John, itself due to the same Semitic idiom.

This use of καί is, however, as good Greek as the preceding ones which Burney attacked. Kühner-Gerth (§ 521, 5) gives several examples from Greek literature; e.g., S. *El.* 1207: πιθοῦ λέγοντι κοὐχ ἁμαρτήσῃ ποτέ. This construction is recognized as good Greek by Lagrange,[3] who quotes Plato *Phaed.* 59e, and cites Euclid iv. 6.

Nor has this usage any lack of attestation in Hellenistic Greek; e.g., P. Teb. II, 283 (petition, 93 or 60 B.C.),

---

[1] Cf. Howard, *op. cit.*, p. 422, and Bauer, *Wörterbuch.*

[2] *Op. cit.*, p. 128.   [3] *Op. cit.*, p. cvii.

lines 12 f.: δέδωκα [l. δέδωκε] αὐτῇ πληγὰς πλήους εἰς τὸ {ἐξ} τυχὸν μέρος τοῦ σώματος καὶ κινδύνωι [l. κινδυνεύει] τῶι ζῆν; Epictetus i. 24. 19: 'ἀλλὰ μακάριος ὁ δεῖνα μετὰ πολλῶν γὰρ περιπατεῖ.' κἀγὼ συγκατατάττω ἐμαυτὸν σὺν τοῖς πολλοῖς καὶ μετὰ πολλῶν περιπατῶ. Compare Epictetus i. 9. 27; 4. 2; 2. 18; P. Oxy. I, 106 (revocation of a will, 135 A.D.), lines 4 f.; P. Oxy, III, 474 (circular to officials, 184 A.D.), lines 33 f., etc.

d) FREQUENCY OF οὖν

The extraordinary frequency of this conjunction in John (as compared with the Synoptics) is regarded by Burney (p. 68) as a reflection of the frequent use of "and" with the sense "and so" in Semitic.

John's use of οὖν 200 times does seem extraordinary when compared with Matthew's 57, Mark's 6, and Luke's 31. It is not quite so startling in comparison with Epictetus' use of it 173 times in i. 1–24, a section which approximates the size of John. The average use in 375 papyri is about the same as the use in Matthew and Luke. But the variation here also is high. Only 57 out of the 375 papyri used οὖν at all, and one of the 57 used it 11 times in 162 lines.

The Semitic influence supposed by Burney seems a conjecture of the most useless sort. Οὖν, he says, represents the Semitic *waw*, meaning "and so." But he argues elsewhere that this is translated in John by καί, and, as has been shown above, καί = "and so" is common in Greek. Why, then, would the translator substitute οὖν? It is true that οὖν also means "and so" in Greek literature,[1]

---

[1] Bernard, *op. cit.*, I, 37; and Liddell and Scott.

But the work of a translator would be evident here only if he used the "and" of his original.

e) Infrequency of δέ

John and Mark use δέ only half as often as Matthew and Luke, and the explanation given by Burney (p. 69) is that Western Aramaic has no equivalent for δέ.

Jannaris[1] regards it as probable that the limited use of this conjunction in the New Testament is the first indication of its retreat from popular speech, a retreat that became complete in the period 600–1000 A.D. Its non-existence in modern colloquial Greek supports the theory that its use was already declining in the New Testament period, in the judgment of Pernot,[2] who regards this as another instance of the more colloquial nature of the Greek of Mark and John.

Some support for this claim may be seen in the relative frequency of δέ in Epictetus and the papyri. Epictetus uses the conjunction more frequently than John does, about 250 times in a section the length of John (as compared with John's 176); yet he is closer to John and Mark than to the First and Third Gospels. On the other hand, δέ occurs in the papyri less frequently than in John, as far as an approximate estimate shows. In the 375 papyri tabulated, it occurs a little over 300 times, which, in view of the estimated size of the papyri, would reduce to an average about as much below John's as Epictetus' is above it.

There is, however, nothing like uniformity in the usage

---

[1] *Op. cit.*, § 1709.   [2] *Op. cit.*, p. 128.

of the papyri. For instance, the 25 papyri that contain δέ
only once range in size from 6 lines to 55 lines. This suggests very forcibly that variation in the frequency of the
use of δέ may depend upon other things than the presence
or absence of Semitic influence.

f) INFREQUENCY OF γάρ

Γάρ is less frequent in John than in the Synoptics, as
Burney (p. 69) says, but a less significant difference could
hardly find a place in a linguistic argument. Using Burney's figures and making all the gospels the length of
Matthew, the occurrences would be Matthew, 125; Mark,
96; Luke, 109; John, 86. It would evidently take a variation of less than ten in a hundred to convince Burney that
there was even approximate agreement in usage. His
argument here demands a too tremendous significance in
any variation between John and any one of the Synoptics.
For, as the figures stand, Mark, Luke, and John agree as
closely as can reasonably be expected of different Greek
authors, and even Matthew (whose variation is the only
noticeable one) is hardly far enough from the others to be
classified apart from them.

In a section of the *Discourses* approximately the same
length as John, there are 99 occurrences of γάρ. This may
be called approximate agreement with Mark, Luke, and
John. In the papyri, γάρ seems to be used less frequently
than in Epictetus and the gospels. In 375 papyri, 76
occurrences of γάρ were counted. That means that γάρ
occurs only about one-third as often in the papyri as in
John. Here also, however, there is variation in usage

among different papyri, of the sort noted above in regard to δέ. Even without this comparison and solely on the basis of Burney's own figures, John's use of γάρ cannot be classified as due to Aramaic influence.

g) FREQUENCY OF ἵνα

Burney's figures (p. 69) for the occurrences of ἵνα in each gospel (each gospel's total being increased so as to make it represent a gospel as long as Matthew) are as follows: Matthew, 33; Mark, 88; Luke, 44; John, 163. The greater frequency in John and Mark, and the fact that Matthew and Luke on eight occasions avoid the ἵνα of Mark, points, in Burney's opinion, to the influence of the Aramaic particle ד, which was used as a relative pronoun, a sign of the genitive, and a conjunction.

The history of the use of ἵνα is a record of rapid expansion in use after 300 B.C., at the expense of ὅπως and ὡς. Jannaris[1] speaks of it as having become "very common—perhaps the commonest word next to καί and the article." There was, however, from 150 B.C. to 300 A.D. some reaction against ἵνα on the part of the literati. Thus its common use or avoidance could occur on other grounds than Semitic influence, and this is shown also by the fact that although "it is Herodotos' favorite [final] particle" and is "fairly frequent in Lucian," yet it is "entirely wanting both in Lucian's typical narrative, *True Histories*, and in the *d.d.S.*"[2] Pernot[3] sees the higher fre-

[1] *Op. cit.*, pp. 416–17.

[2] D. A. Penick, *Gildersleeve Studies*, pp. 390–91.

[3] Op. cit., p. 128.

quency in John as another sign of the more "vulgar" quality of John's Greek. Yet both Epictetus and the papyri use ἵνα only one sixth as frequently as John does.

h) FREQUENCY OF ἵνα μή

The occurrences of ἵνα μή, as given by Burney (p. 69), are as follows: Matthew, 8; Mark, 5; Luke, 8; John, 18. The relative frequency in John is, in his opinion, due to Aramaic influence.

John's use is, however, merely a development of classical usage:

The history of the Greek language shows a gradual decrease of final μή and an increase of the final particles with μή in negative final clauses. The tendency in this direction was so strong that ὅπως μή sometimes took the place of μή even after verbs of *fearing*, to express the object of the fear, while it became the regular form after verbs of *striving*, etc., to express the object aimed at.[1]

This statement of Goodwin's, which covers classical usage only, would be equally valid for the Koine if ἵνα were substituted for ὅπως in his sentence as it actually was in Koine usage.

Ἵνα μή is not as frequent in Epictetus or the papyri as it is in John. In Epictetus it occurs with about half the frequency of John, and in the papyri still more infrequently. But lest this should be taken as ample justification for the assumption that John was translated from an Aramaic gospel, it should be noted that "ἵνα μή is found twice as often in the Pauline Epistles as in John."[2]

[1] Goodwin, *op. cit.*, p. 112.
[2] Allis, *op. cit.*, p. 562.

i) ἵνα μή (INSTEAD OF μήποτε) = "LEST"

Burney (p. 100) sees significance in the fact that ἵνα
μή is used in John to mean "lest," while μήποτε, which he
seems to regard as the only normal way of expressing
"lest" in Greek, never occurs in John or the Apocalypse.

The difference in use between "lest" and "that not" is
not much sharper in Greek than in English, the clearest
examples of "lest" occurring after verbs of fearing. Burney can find no such use of ἵνα μή in John. But even if in
the passages he cites ἵνα μή actually did mean "lest," that
would not set John apart from Greek usage. An equivalent construction (see above) was already current in
classical Greek, and John's use of ἵνα μή can easily be
paralleled from Hellenistic Greek; e.g., iii. 24. 81: οὐκ
ἀρνήσῃ καὶ ὅσα ἔμαθες εἰδέναι, ἵνα μὴ διαβάλῃς τὰ θεωρήματα
ὡς ἄχρηστα, which Mrs. Carter translates, "for fear of
bringing a scandal upon theorems as useless"; and P.
Oxy. X, 1294 (letter, ii/iii A.D.), lines 12 f.: [μελη]σάτω
δέ σοι τῶν ἐν τῷ χειλώματι ἵνα μὴ σαπῇ, which is translated
by the editors, "lest they rot."

And nothing could more clearly characterize John as
popular Hellenistic Greek than the absence of μήποτε =
"lest." It is absent from the Pauline epistles, says Allis
(p. 562). Not a single occurrence was found in the non-
literary papyri of the Roman period in the twenty-four
volumes of papyri covered in this study. And it was noted
but once in the *Discourses* of Epictetus, in iv. 13. 4, the
last chapter of the last book.

Burney concludes his treatment of ἵνα μή and μήποτε
with the claim that the use of ἵνα μή in John 12:40 proves

that John is translated from Aramaic, as distinct from Hebrew. The proof, as he sees it, lies in the fact that John in this quotation from the Old Testament abandons the μήποτε which the Septuagint here (Isa. 6:10) uses to translate the Hebrew פֶּן = "lest," and substitutes ἵνα μή = "that not" in agreement with the Syriac of the Peshitto. Moreover, Matthew and Mark use μήποτε in the same quotation. And so Burney asks (p. 100), "What evidence could prove more cogently that his [John's] Greek translates an Aramaic original?"

The cogency of this proof is weakened by a more extensive study of the use of ἵνα μή in translation and composition Greek. Allis (p. 562) has pointed out that it translates the Hebrew פֶּן 11 times in the Septuagint in the Pentateuch, and Howard (p. 470) calls attention to Dr. Charles' argument that Hebrew, *not* Aramaic, is the background of Revelation where μήποτε never occurs and ἵνα μή occurs 11 times. When one remembers also the overwhelming evidence cited above for the relative frequency of ἵνα μή and infrequency of μήποτε to express "lest" in Hellenistic Greek, the cogency of this proof that John's Greek translates not only a Semitic but an Aramaic original becomes almost a minus quantity.

CHAPTER IV

MISTRANSLATIONS

A list of "mistranslations" of the original Aramaic in John is furnished by each of the Semitic scholars whose arguments have been followed in this study. Burney's list, which is taken up first here, was regarded by Burney himself as essential to his argument. He prefaces his chapter on mistranslations as follows:

> The most weighty form of evidence in proof that a document is a translation from another language is the existence of difficulties or peculiarities of language which can be shown to find their solution in the theory of mistranslation from the assumed original language.[1]

It is to be noted that it is linguistic difficulties and peculiarities which lead him to the claim of mistranslation.

MISTRANSLATIONS ALLEGED BY BURNEY

1. ἵνα FOR דְּ = "WHO"

"The actual *mistranslation* of an original Aramaic document" seemed to Burney (pp. 75 f.) the only possible explanation of the use of ἵνα in half a dozen Johannine passages: 1:8, 5:7, 6:30, 6:50, 9:36, 14:16. For most of these Burney presents no further evidence than a translation into Syriac or Aramaic in which the conjunctive particle could carry the relative meaning. But for 1:8 he notes that retranslation into Aramaic makes the ellipse

[1] *Aramaic Origin of the Fourth Gospel*, p. 101.

unnecessary; for 9:36, that the translation of ἵνα as "who" raises the quality of the man's faith. And the clinching evidence for his argument he finds in the fact that the ἵνα of Mark 4:22 is reproduced in Matt. 10:26 and Luke 8:17 by ὅ. In regard to John 6:30, he admits that the final sense is as natural in Aramaic as in Greek; so he does not press the evidence of this passage. He might well have said that the final sense was natural in Greek in 6:50, 14:16, 1:8, and (if he had treated the passage linguistically) 9:36.[1]

Burrows[2] "sees no clear evidence of translation" in 5:7, and in general feels that the interpretations Burney suggests are no better than the readings of the text. But he is impressed by the cumulative nature of Burney's argument. Much the same position is taken by Torrey.[3]

That ἵνα had more than a final use in Hellenistic Greek is well known; and there are passages in which it is the practical equivalent of ὅς; e.g., Epictetus i. 24. 3: οὐδεὶς δὲ δειλὸν κατάσκοπον πέμπει, ἵν', ἂν μόνον ἀκούσῃ ψόφου καὶ σκιάν ποθεν ἴδῃ, τρέχων ἔλθῃ τεταραγμένος καὶ λέγων ἤδη παρεῖναι τοὺς πολεμίους. Mrs. Carter here translates ἵνα with "who," as she does in iv. 1. 108. And in the following passage the ἵνα is used exactly like the Semitic indeclinable relative pronoun, for it is completed by a per-

[1] In five of these six passages Goguel ("Une nouvelle théorie sur l'origine du quatrième évangile," *Revue d'histoire et de philosophie religieuses*, 1923, pp. 373–82) prefers the final force of ἵνα.

[2] "The Original Language of the Gospel of John," *Journal of Biblical Literature*, XLIX, 128 f.

[3] "The Aramaic Origin of the Gospel of John," *Harvard Theological Review*, XVI, p. 328.

sonal pronoun; moreover, the translation of ἵν' . . . .
αὐτῷ as "whom" makes good sense: iv. 3. 9: ἐλεύθερος
γάρ εἰμι καὶ φίλος τοῦ θεοῦ, ἵν' ἑκὼν πείθωμαι αὐτῷ. And
Howard[1] cites Melcher's opinion that the ἵνα of Encheiridion 51 is used as a relative. Obviously a use of ἵνα that
invites translation by a relative is known to Hellenistic
Greek.

Burney's argument from the Syriac versions and the
reconstruction of an Aramaic text has been challenged
vigorously. His claim that if the passages in John were
translated "into Aramaic in the only possible way, representing ἵνα by ‏ד‎, ... an Aramaic scholar would, without question, give to that ‏ד‎ the sense 'who' or 'which,' "
will not stand in the face of the following facts: In some
of these passages (6:30, 50 etc.), "Burkitt renders the de
of Cur. Sin. by 'that.' "[2] The Latin translation of the
Peshitto by Gwilliam has ut where these passages have
ἵνα, except for 5:7.[3] G. R. Driver regards Burney's claim
as unnecessary in every case, and asks why the Septuagint does not mistranslate the Hebrew indeclinable relative.[4] And Lagrange sees nothing to hinder the translation of ἵνα in 5:7 with final force.[5]

Nor are Burney's other statements any more convincing. The elimination of the ellipse in 1:8 is not at all
necessary for the sake of the Greek.[6] It is common with

[1] *Grammar of New Testament Greek*, II, 436.

[2] Noted by Allis, "The Alleged Aramaic Origin of the Fourth Gospel,"
Princeton Theological Review, XXVI, p. 539.

[3] Noted by Lagrange, *S. Jean*, p. cix.

[4] *Original Language*, p. 3.   [5] *Op. cit.*

[6] Pernot, *Rêvue des études grecques*, XXXVII, 127; Allis, *op. cit.*, p. 537.

ἀλλ’ ἵνα in John.[1] Blass-Debrunner[2] finds nothing remarkable in such a construction. It is found in Epictetus; e.g., i. 17. 18.

The facts in regard to the passages in John which Burney cited may be summarized as follows: (1) In no case is the relative force of ἵνα inescapable;[3] in most cases a final force is preferable. (2) The uses of ἵνα cited by Burney are good Greek; parallel uses can be found in Hellenistic Greek. (3) Authorities on the Semitic languages do not translate these same clauses in Syriac as relative clauses; and several refuse to indorse Burney's claims. This makes a fourth fact obvious: (4) Burney failed to establish this use of ἵνα as a mistranslation.

2. ἵνα = "When"

In John 12:23; 13:1; 16:2, 32, Burney (p. 78) regards ἵνα as a mistranslation of "when," more strictly speaking relatival "which," with ellipsis of "in it." He seems to feel that the alternatives are "when" and "the mystic final sense postulated by Westcott"! It should be noted that in each case ἵνα follows ὥρα.

Torrey (p. 328) is skeptical as to the force of this argument for translation. His skepticism is based on a knowledge of the "loose use" of ἵνα in Hellenistic Greek which gave it many another than a mystic final sense.[4] One of these various uses was as the equivalent of an infinitive

---

[1] Cf. Abbott, *Johannine Grammar*, §§ 2106 f.

[2] *Neutestamentliche Grammatik*[5], § 448, 7.

[3] Bernard, *St. John*, I, 10, regards each of Burney's corrections as "unnecessary."

[4] Cf. Moulton, *Prolegomena*, pp. 206–10.

clause, and Allis (p. 545) recognizes that use here.[1] No
exact parallel in Epictetus to this construction after ὥρα
has been found, but the use of ἵνα with the subjunctive
as a substitute for the infinitive is, of course, quite common. Howard's summary (p. 470) is a fair statement of
the case and will perhaps suffice here since so much space
has been given to the similar uses of ἵνα in other sections
of this study.

Mr. G. R. Driver cites several instances from late Greek of
καιρὸς ἔρχεται (ἐστιν) ἵνα; whilst MGr. εἶνε καιρὸς νὰ ἔλθῃς is the
regular idiom for "it is time for you to come." To this we may add,
ἦρθεν ἡ ὥρα νὰ πεθάνῃ, "the hour came to die" (Thumb Hdb. 187).
This usage is therefore at most a secondary Semitism, and can
quite as easily be explained by the writer's strong partiality for
this particle, which had already gained great flexibility in the
Κοινή.

3. ὅτι = "WHEN"

This mistranslation is found by Burney (p. 78) in two
passages in John: 9:8 and 12:41; here, he feels, "the
natural inference is that ד = 'when' has been wrongly interpreted as conjunctive 'that.' "

In neither of these passages does Burney's explanation
seem necessary.[2] Allis (p. 545) has suggested that in 9:8
the ὅτι is simply the equivalent of an accusative with
the infinitive.[3] And Howard (p. 469) quotes from Mr.
G. R. Driver a close parallel to this Johannine passage,
taken from late Greek. In regard to the second passage,

---

[1] Cf. Jannaris, *Historical Greek Grammar*, § 1758; Blass-Debrunner,
op. cit., §§ 369, 382.

[2] Lagrange, *S. Jean, loc. cit.*, notices no difficulty.

[3] Cf. Blass-Debrunner, *op. cit.*, § 408; Epictetus ii. 18. 32.

Howard feels that Burney's explanation is unnecessary. This "late Greek usage" persisted into modern Greek, and M. Pernot has claimed that the modern Greek which replaced ὅτι by πῶς or ποῦ, would employ in these Johannine passages one or the other of these forms.[1]

That a use of ὅτι which could be translated "when" was not unknown to Hellenistic Greek is shown by the following passages from Epictetus, in each of which Mrs. Carter translated the ὅτι by "when": ii. 14. 21: καίτοι τί σοι ἐγὼ κακὸν πεποίηκα; εἰ μὴ καὶ τὸ ἔσοπτρον τῷ αἰσχρῷ, ὅτι δεικνύει αὐτὸν αὐτῷ οἷός ἐστιν· . . . . ; and ii. 18. 31 similarly.

This is not to say that either in John or in Epictetus the ὅτι must be translated "when," but only to show that an unprejudiced translator of Hellenistic Greek could regard ὅτι as equivalent to "when." As a matter of fact, the translation suggested by Burney for these passages has obviously no advantage over a translation that does not regard ὅτι as representing "when," nor is there any difficulty in the Greek. This "mistranslation" falls with many others into that class where the argument rests solely upon the fact that if the passage were translated into Aramaic, two meanings would be possible.

4. ὅτι = דְּ , "Who"

Here we find one of the few agreements among those who argue for the Aramaic origin of John. Burney (pp. 76 f.) and Montgomery[2] both regard the ὅτι in John 8. 45.

[1] *Op. cit.*, p. 128.

[2] *The Origin of the Gospel According to St. John*, p. 31.

as a mistranslation of the Aramaic ך="who." Burney makes the same claim for ὅτι in John 9:17 and 1:16, and points out that the Syriac particle which is used in these passages in the Syriac versions may have a relative sense. Burrows (pp. 128 f.) sees little force in Burney's claim for 9:17, but regards his case in regard to 8:45 as a strong one.

But the Greek relative was often used with causal force, even in classical Greek,[1] and it therefore follows that ὅτι frequently appears where ὅς would cause no difficulty in the Greek.

A large number of passages could be quoted from Hellenistic Greek in which ὅτι could be translated as a relative and has been translated as a relative; e.g., Epictetus i. 29. 49: ταῦτα μέλλεις μαρτυρεῖν καὶ καταισχύνειν τὴν κλῆσιν ἣν κέκληκεν, ὅτι σε ἐτίμησεν ταύτην τὴν τιμὴν καὶ ἄξιον ἡγήσατο προσαγαγεῖν εἰς μαρτυρίαν τηλικαύτην; Epictetus iii. 1. 37: τὸν ἄνθρωπον ποιήσει λέγειν σοι ταῦτα, ἵν' ἀγνοῇς τὴν δύναμιν τοῦ δαιμονίου, ὅτι τοῖς μὲν οὕτως, τοῖς δ' ἐκείνως σημαίνει, ... Mrs. Carter translates ὅτι in these two passages as a relative. BGU II, 423 (letter, ii A.D.), lines 6 f.: Εὐχαριστῶ τῷ κυρίῳ Σεράπιδι, ὅτι μου κινδυνεύσαντος εἰς θάλασσαν ἔσωσε εὐθέως. Compare also Epictetus ii. 15. 18; iii. 1. 20; iv. 7. 21; 10. 5; 11. 23; P. Oxy. I, 113 (letter, ii A.D.), line 27.

It should be clearly understood that this is not to argue that ὅτι in the passages in John *should* be translated as a relative, but only that passages in which ὅτι can be translated as a relative occur in the unquestioned

[1] For discussion and examples, cf. p. 105.

Greek writings contemporaneous with John; and that, therefore, such occurrences in John cannot be of much value as evidences of mistranslation. For, if it were to be shown that the translation as a relative would be superior, this would not, considering the passages cited above, make recourse to the theory of an Aramaic original necessary.

5. ($\pi\hat{\alpha}\nu$) $\ddot{o}$ = דְּ, "WHO"

The relative has been recognized as a mistranslation by Burney (pp. 101 f.) in John 10:29, 17:11, 17:12, 17:24, 17:2, 6:37, 6:39. The use of the neuter gender of the relative here instead of the masculine is explained by Burney as due to the genderless Aramaic relative, and for the last three passages he refers to the Hebrew כֻּלּוֹ = "the whole of it" or "all of them," whose "neutral suffix" is faithfully reproduced by John.

Kühner-Gerth describes classical usage (§ 361, 2) as follows:

The relative often occurs, without reference to the gender of its substantive, in the neuter singular when the substantive is regarded not as an individual but as a general concept; e.g., S. Or. 542; Eur. Hel. 1687; Pl. Conv. 196, a; *ibid.* 3, 104.

Similarly in Hellenistic Greek, the neuter singular relative often refers to an antecedent of a different gender or number; e.g., Epictetus ii. 14. 3: $\kappa\alpha\grave{\iota}$ $\tau\grave{\alpha}$ $\mu\grave{\epsilon}\nu$ $\dot{\alpha}\pi\grave{o}$ $\tau\hat{\omega}\nu$ $\tau\epsilon\chi\nu\hat{\omega}\nu$ $\gamma\iota\nu\acute{o}\mu\epsilon\nu\alpha$ $\tau\acute{\eta}\nu$ $\tau\epsilon$ $\chi\rho\epsilon\acute{\iota}\alpha\nu$ $\epsilon\dot{v}\theta\grave{v}s$ $\dot{\epsilon}\nu\delta\epsilon\acute{\iota}\kappa\nu\upsilon\tau\alpha\iota$ $\pi\rho\grave{o}s$ $\dot{o}$ $\gamma\acute{\epsilon}\gamma o\nu\epsilon\nu$ . . . . ; P. Lond. II, 142 (receipt, 95 A.D.), line 7: $\delta\rho\alpha\chi\mu\alpha s$ $\chi\epsilon\iota\lambda\iota\alpha s$ $\delta\iota\alpha\kappa o\sigma\iota\alpha s$ $\tau\epsilon\sigma\sigma\alpha\rho\alpha\kappa o\nu\tau\alpha$ $\kappa\alpha\iota$ $\tau o[\upsilon]s$ $\tau o\upsilon\tau\omega\nu$ $\tau o\kappa o\upsilon s$ α $\omega\phi\iota\lambda\epsilon\nu$ $\alpha\upsilon\tau\omega\iota$.

There is no space in a work of this kind to take up

each of these passages in John in detail and argue from the exegetical viewpoint for or against Burney's claims.[1] It may be worth noting, however, that in the half a dozen passages cited by Burney as examples in the Hebrew Old Testament of the Semitic idiom behind the last three Johannine passages, the Septuagint never translates the "Hebrew neutral suffix" by a neuter singular; πάντες and πᾶς τις occur, but not πᾶν ὅ. If there is, formally, no neuter gender in Semitic, what led the "translator" of John to choose the neuter gender in these passages?

Πᾶν ὅ occurs in Epictetus where a masculine might have seemed more appropriate; e.g., iii. 15. 6: οὕτως καὶ σὺ νῦν μὲν ἀθλητής, νῦν δὲ μονομάχος, εἶτα φιλόσοφος, εἶτα ῥήτωρ, ὅλη δὲ τῇ ψυχῇ οὐδέν, ἀλλ᾽ ὡς ὁ πίθηκος πᾶν ὅ ἂν ἴδῃς μιμῇ. . . . .[2] It may be that what led John to use the neuter with πᾶν was the naturalness of the construction to one writing in Greek, for Howard (p. 437) has shown by citing I John 5:4 that πᾶν ὅ was used in a collective sense in "composition" Greek.

6. ὅς = דְּ, "Because"

Burney (pp. 29, 34) thinks that the Greek relative in John 1:4 and 1:13 is a mistranslation of the Aramaic דְּ, which sometimes, as here, had causal force. In 1:13, he thus finds the author of the gospel "drawing out the mystical import of the Virgin birth for believers."

One cannot escape the impression that there is something more than linguistic interest behind such an argu-

---

[1] Cf. Abbott, *op. cit.*, §§ 1921, 2422. Goguel, *op. cit.*, p. 379 n., regards all these passages save 10: 29 as simply constructions *ad sensum*.

[2] For further examples, cf. Schenkl's Index.

ment; there is certainly nothing "difficult" or "peculiar" in the Greek. In the first instance cited, the argument about the point of sentence division may have suggested the mistranslation to Burney. In neither instance does Howard (p. 436) feel that there is any necessity for this explanation of the relative pronoun. And Allis (p. 544) has noted that "the Syriac versions clearly support the reading of the Greek, except that the uncertainty as to the point of division between verses 3 and 4 makes the Peshitto ambiguous."

But if it were true that in each of these passages the Greek relative carried a causal force, that would be no argument against regarding the passages as composition Greek. For this use of the relative pronoun is well attested for classical Greek by Goodwin,[1] who quotes Herodotus i. 33: Δόξας ἀμαθέα εἶναι, ὅς . . . . ἐκέλευε, "believing him to be unlearned, because he commanded," with many other passages from Greek literature. That this construction is also found in Hellenistic Greek is shown by the following example from the *Discourses:* ii. 6. 20: ἐγὼ δ' οὐ κινδυνεύω, ὃς οἰκῶ ἐν Νικοπόλει, ὅπου σεισμοὶ τοσοῦτοι; . . . . .

It would seem, then, that whether the relative in the Johannine passages quoted by Burney has a causal force or not, there is nothing in it that is unusual as Greek.

7. ἕν FOR "THIS"

This is yet another instance in which Burney ignored the definition of mistranslation which he himself estab-

---

[1] *Moods and Tenses*, p. 220; cf. Kühner-Gerth, *op. cit.*, § 554.

lished. He suggests (p. 112) that the ἓν οἶδα of John 9:25 is an erroneous rendering of an Aramaic phrase meaning "this I know," which is actually the reading of Palestinian Syriac here. He admits, however, that the present text yields a suitable sense. And since he advances no argument for his hypothetical Aramaic original as yielding a more suitable sense, and does not attack the possibility of ἓν οἶδα as good Greek, the weakness of his position is apparent.

8. τὰ ῥήματα = "THE THINGS"

John 6:63, τὰ ῥήματα ἃ ἐγὼ λελάληκα ὑμῖν, seems to Burney (pp. 108 f.) to mean "the things about which I have been speaking to you."[1] He makes this claim because of the fact that in Aramaic as in Hebrew one word means both "word" and "thing"; and also because the Septuagint and Theodotion frequently translate this ambiguous Semitic word by ῥῆμα = "thing."

This very frequency is one of the arguments against Burney's position. In less than fifteen chapters of Genesis ῥῆμα = "thing" occurs at least half a dozen times. But, in John, Burney claims but this one passage, and "perhaps" 6:68.

Another argument against Burney's claim lies in the nature of the verb with which ῥῆμα is used in John. For, although in the Septuagint and Theodotion there are clear uses of ῥῆμα in Semitic fashion with verbs which demand "thing" as their object, no such use occurs in John.

---

[1] Liddell and Scott gives as a second meaning for ῥῆμα: "the thing spoken of, a thing."

And so Burney is driven to suspect ῥῆμα of meaning "thing" when it is the object of a verb of speaking! With what sort of a verb would he expect ῥῆμα to be used so as to mean "word"?

9. ἦν = "HE"

"John 1:9: ἦν τὸ φῶς τὸ ἀληθινόν can only mean," says Burney (p. 33), " 'It was the true light,' referring to the preceding verse. For this sense we seem to need a demonstrative pronoun; and this probably stood in Aramaic as הוּא which was misread as הֲרָא and rendered ἦν." Torrey (p. 329) says of Burney's suggestion here that "it seems most improbable because of the preceding verse. His conjectured הוּא would naturally refer to John the Baptist, even in the text which he restores."

Allis (p. 564) points out that there can be no question of the correctness of ἦν τὸ φῶς, which is not attacked by Burney; and it does not seem necessary to quote passages to illustrate such a common Greek construction. Burney has not established mistranslation in this passage.

10. IMPERFECT FOR PLUPERFECT

In regard to the imperfect in John 2:22, ἐμνήσθησαν οἱ μαθηταὶ αὐτοῦ ὅτι τοῦτο ἔλεγεν, Burney (p. 108) says: "We note the curious use of the imperfect . . . . where the context demands a pluperfect." This is due, he thinks, to the fact that it translates the Aramaic "he had said," which in the unvocalized text was confused by the translator with "he was saying."

An imperfect in indirect discourse after a verb of remembering would not seem strange to Greek ears, for it is a rule of Hellenistic Greek grammar that in indirect discourse the verb keeps the tense of the direct. Several other factors would make this sound natural to Greek readers of the gospel: in the first place, the "never robust" pluperfect tense was becoming more and more of a rarity; in the second, the imperfect of λέγω was often used without any thought of expressing continuing action.[1] All this leads Pernot to say: "It is not correct to say that the use of the imperfect in place of the pluperfect . . . . is surprising. It would be surprising, on the contrary, to find the pluperfect used here."[2]

11. καταλαμβάνω FOR "DARKEN"

In regard to the use of this verb in 1:5 and 12:35, Burney (pp. 29 f.) follows the suggestion of Dr. Ball "that confusion may have arisen in Aramaic between the Aph'el form 'aḳbēl, darken' and the Pa'el form ḳabbēl 'receive,' 'take.'" Torrey (p. 329) rejects this: "In 1, 5 and 12, 35 (even without the added difficulty of supposing that the same rather unlikely blunder was made twice), ... I very decidedly prefer the present readings to those which Burney proposes." This preference is shared by Bernard[3] and Allis (p. 563), who point out that the argument is not based on grammatical form but on subject matter, and that John's usage is easily paralleled in Greek writings outside the New Testament.[4] Thus Driver (*Original Lan-*

---

[1] Cf. above, p. 29.   [2] *Op. cit.*, p. 128.   [3] *Op. cit.*, I, 6.

[4] Field, *Notes, etc.*, p. 84, quotes Herodotus i. 87 in which Blakesly finds the meaning "extinguish" for this verb. Cf. W. Bauer, *Wörterbuch*, and *Das Johannesevangelium* on 1:5.

guage) points out that "Diodorus Siculus was not mis-translating Aramaic when he wrote τῆς νυκτὸς καταλαβού-σης (xx. 86)"; and that "the same verb is used of ἀμέρα (Dittenberger, *Sylloge* 803, 14) and of νόσος (Pap. Oxyrh. VI 939, 5)." Epictetus also uses it of νόσος and θάνατος in iii. 5. 5, 11.

There can be no doubt of the soundness of Burrows' judgment that "Burney has been led astray by Ball's theory that κατέλαβεν is a mistranslation."[1]

12. JOHN 7:37–38

With the supposition that "belly" was read by mistake for the very similar Aramaic word "fountain," and by re-dividing the clauses, Burney (pp. 109 f.) secures the following as the original meaning of this passage: "He that thirsteth, let him come unto me; and let him drink that believeth in me. As the Scripture hath said, 'Rivers shall flow forth from the fountain of living waters.' "

Torrey (p. 329) says of this, "But Burney's restored Aramaic is too far removed from the Greek, too improbable in itself, and not sufficiently like anything in the Old Testament." "Dr. G. B. Gray has pertinently pointed out that Burney has forgotten the pronoun αὐτοῦ";[2] and Goguel claims that Burney's explanation sacrifices the Johannine thought (as in the interview with the Samaritan woman) that the living water comes from within, not from without.[3]

---

[1] "The Johannine Prologue as Aramaic Verse," *Journal of Biblical Literature*, XLV (1926), 61.

[2] Driver, *op. cit.*   [3] *Op. cit.*, p. 380.

Torrey's own assumption (pp. 339 f.) is that מִבְּוָה was read by error for מִבַּוָּה, and that the original read: ". . . . As the Scripture hath said, 'Out of the midst of her (i.e., Jerusalem) shall flow rivers of living water.' " Howard (p. 475) refers to still another conjectured Semitic original, suggested by Rendel Harris; and also calls attention to explanations by W. E. Barnes and H. St. J. Thackeray which "dispense with any emendations of the Greek text."

The various Semitic originals suggested for this passage are about on a par; there is some degree of possibility in all of them; there is nothing compelling in any of them. Torrey's reconstruction is also "too improbable in itself." Lagrange has pointed out[1] that his reconstruction drags Jerusalem into a context with which it has nothing to do; and Burrows (p. 133) cannot see why the original writer should have substituted "her" for "Jerusalem."

Difficulties in the text of an ancient document do not demand the theory of mistranslation;[2] it is only when that theory clears up the difficulties in a most convincing fashion that the theory is justified; and that that is not the case here is obvious.

13. Οἴδαμεν FOR "I KNOW"

"The strange use of οἴδαμεν, 20:2, in the mouth of Mary Magdalen, where we should expect οὐκ οἶδα, may

[1] *S. Jean* on 7:37–38.

[2] Interestingly enough, Epictetus' translators have found difficulty in a passage in which he uses the word κοιλία, ii. 16. 44. Cf. Mrs. Carter's translation and note; also Long's translation, and Upton's and Oldfather's text.

be due to a misreading as 1st plural perfect of an original feminine singular participle combined with 1st personal pronoun." Burney, who gives this explanation (pp. 112 f.), suggests its possibility for the same phenomenon in John 3:2.

Torrey, however (p. 329), regards this plural as correct Semitic usage, and admits that this substitution of plural for singular is well known in Greek. So also Burrows (p. 114): "Burney's supposition that the singular has been incorrectly pointed as the plural in v. 2 is quite gratuitous."

Practically every grammar and Greek syntax yields examples from classical Greek of the use of the plural for the singular.[1] Gildersleeve gives numerous examples from the first person in which "the particular is sunk in the generic, the individual in the class, the woman in her male kindred."[2] The same condition exists in Hellenistic Greek. K. Dick has given some examples from Hellenistic literature and from the papyri,[3] which in Moulton's judgment prove "that 'I' and 'we' chased each other throughout these documents without rhyme or reason."[4]

The rapid interchange of singular and plural in the *Discourses* surpasses anything in John. i. 5. 3–5 uses "we" throughout; i. 5. 6–10 uses "I." i. 6. 37 begins, Ἄγε οὖν καὶ σὺ τούτων αἰσθόμενος ἀπόβλεψον . . . . and continues in

---

[1] Kühner-Gerth, *op. cit.*, § 371, 3; Blass, *Grammar*, § 48, 4 (cited by Torrey).

[2] *Greek Syntax*, I, 27.

[3] *Der schriftstellerische Plural bei Paulus* (Halle, 1900), pp. 15–32.

[4] *Op. cit.*, p. 86.

the singular; but i. 6. 38 begins abruptly οὔ· ἀλλὰ κάθησθε
and continues in the plural. Note the change from plural
to singular in i. 30. 6–7, and from singular to plural in the
same sentence in i. 1. 12.[1]

To the passages cited from the papyri by Milligan[2] to
prove that the two numbers could be used interchange-
ably, the following may be added: P. Oxy. XII, 1479
(letter, i B.C.), lines 2 f.: ἐκομισάμην εἴληφ(α) . . . .
[ε]ἰρήκαμεν . . . . , translated as "I received . . . . I ob-
tained . . . . I told . . . . " by the editors. P. Oxy. VII,
1061 (letter, 22 B.C.), lines 1 f.: Διογέν[η]s Διονυσίωι τῶι
ἀδελφῶι . . . . ἐπειδὴι καὶ ἄλλοτέ σοι ἐγράψαμεν . . . .
διαφέρετε . . . . ἔγραψα. Compare P. Lond. II, 331 (tem-
porary appointment, 165 A.D.), lines 12 f.; BGU II, 449
(letter, ii/iii A.D.), lines 4 f.; P. Oxy. II, 298 (letter, i
A.D.); P. Oxy. XIV, 1761 (letter, ii/iii A.D.); P. Oxy. XII,
1481 (letter, ii A.D.), line 6.

When to the various uses of the plural for singular
which have been mentioned and illustrated here one adds
that identification of the evangelist with the Christian
community which is found in John,[3] it is not surprising
that in some passages in John the plural should be used
for the singular.[4]

[1] For other passages in Epictetus, cf. Dick, *op. cit.*

[2] *Thessalonians* (London, 1908), pp. 131 f.; cf. Moulton and Milligan,
Vocabulary, s.v. ἐγώ.

[3] Cf. Bernard, *op. cit.*, I, 110.

[4] Goguel (*op. cit.*, p. 380) prefers with Bauer the influence of Matt.
28:1, in which two women come to the sepulcher. The Synoptics also
offer a parallel to the other instance of this plural in John.

14. Change from Direct to Indirect Speech

In John 20:18, Burney (p. 113) finds the change from direct to oblique oration strange and awkward. With the supposition that the Aramaic was read with the wrong vowels, he makes both clauses indirect.[1]

The change from indirect to direct discourse, and more infrequently from direct to indirect, was known to classical Greek; e.g., Xenophon *Anabasis* vii. 1. 39: ἐλθὼν δ' ὁ Κλέανδρος· Μάλα μόλις, ἔφη, διαπραξάμενος ἥκω· λέγειν γὰρ 'Αναξίβιον, ὅτι οὐκ ἐπιτήδειον εἴη κτλ.[2] This may explain why Walter Bauer found here no difficulty demanding explanation, a fact which Torrey is willing to accept as guaranty of the quality of the Greek.

15. John 8:56

No extension of the use of ἵνα seemed to Burney (p. 111) adequate to explain ἠγαλλιάσατο ἵνα ἴδῃ, and he felt that the similarity of the following clause demanded some such meaning as "longed" for ἠγαλλιάσατο. This he found in a Syriac verb, not known to occur in Western Aramaic, which carried both the meaning "longed" and "exulted."

The repetition in the following clause struck Torrey (pp. 340 f.) as a tautology that could not have been in the original. But since "the verb which Burney supposes here is not known to have occurred in Western Aramaic, and (if its use was like that in Syriac) would not easily have

---

[1] Torrey, *op. cit.*, p. 330, regards the texts of 20:18 as correct Semitic usage. This would take it out of the "mistranslation" class.

[2] Kühner-Gerth, *op. cit.*, § 595, 5; Blass-Debrunner, *op. cit.*, § 470; Winer-Moulton, *Grammar of New Testament Greek*[9], p. 725.

been misunderstood," he refuses Burney's reconstruction and resorts to the textual history of the Aramaic gospel of John to solve the problem. The author wrote בעא אברהם, "Abraham prayed"; then the final א of בעא "was omitted in copying, partly because of the immediately following א, partly because 'Abraham exulted to see my day' seemed such a probable saying." This rests on several assumptions: first, that what was impossible for the author would have seemed "such a probable saying" to the copyist; second, the occurrence of the form בע in Palestine in the first century A.D.[1]

The use of ἵνα after verbs of wishing, striving, etc., is regarded by Bauer as sufficient to explain the passage: he translates ἠγαλλιάσατο, "jubelnd streben nach."[2] And further justification of the Johannine passage as Greek is to be seen in the following passages from the papyri: BGU IV, 1081 (letter, iii A.D.), line 5: ἐχάρην, ἵνα σὲ ἀσπάζομαι; Pap. Giess, 17, line 5 (ii A.D.): ἠγωνίασα .... ἵνα ἀκούσω.[3] These examples and the established wide use of ἵνα in the Koine make it possible to agree with Howard (p. 476) that "in any case Burney's suspicion of an Aramaism in the ἵνα-clause is needless."

There remains as an argument against the Greek of this passage only the claim that the author would not have been guilty of such tautology. But such repetition is one

---

[1] Lagrange, S. Jean, loc. cit., says, "But if the form בע had existed, it would nevertheless be astonishing that it should replace in the mind of the translator a very common and suitable form."

[2] Wörterbuch, s.v.

[3] Quoted by Bauer, Das Johannesevangelium, on 8:56.

of the outstanding characteristics of the author's style; cf. 3:31; 6:53–59; etc. Montgomery, in calling attenton (p. 21) to the tautology in John 12:49, τί εἴπω καὶ τί λαλήσω, admits that "rhetorical parallelism, charactcristic of the Semitic, might explain the duplication. . . . ."[1] If repetition here is characteristically Semitic, it cannot be impossible (as Torrey thinks) in 8:56. This disagreement discredits both these arguments. The explanation of 12:49 is, of course, the same as that of 8:56; 3:31, etc., where the author of the Fourth Gospel shows his fondness for repetitious phrases.[2]

MISTRANSLATIONS ALLEGED BY MONTGOMERY

16. JOHN 11:54, ἐν τοῖς Ἰουδαίοις

This phrase seems to Montgomery (p. 21) to stand for "in Judea": "The Peshitto Syriac uses here the idiomatic phrase, *beth Iudaye*, 'in the house,' i.e. 'the land of the Jews'. . . . . For *beth* the translator may have read or understood *be*, 'in,' and so produced 'in the Jews.' "

Gildersleeve's discussion suggests that the same construction was known in classical Greek:

The name of the inhabitants is sometimes used instead of the city: καὶ κρατήσαντες τοῦ ἐν Δελφοῖς ἱεροῦ παρέδοσαν Δελφοῖς,

---

[1] But he prefers to explain it as a doublet in translation.

[2] Burney's treatment of 1:29 has not been taken up here as he has no criticism of the Greek as Greek. The attitude of Montgomery on mistranslations differs from that of Burney. As his thesis does not demand a written Aramaic original for John, he prefaces his list of mistranslations with a cautious statement pointing out that the establishment of mistranslations is not essential to his position. In his argument, other criteria are more important.

Thucydides 1, 112, 5; And having made themselves masters of the sanctuary at Delphi (among the Delphians), they handed it over to the Delphians.

Demosthenes 25, 34: ἐν Δελφοῖς, and similarly often.

Xenophon *Anabasis* 1, 2, 24: ἐν Σόλοις, καὶ ἐν Ἰσσοῖς.[1]

The same construction after the prepositions ἐκ and ἐς is amply illustrated by the same author from the writings of Isocrates, Plato, Herodotus, Demosthenes, and Thucydides.

Walter Bauer translates this phrase in 11:54 by "among the Jews," and has no note of any difficulty in the Greek;[2] and the same is true of Lagrange's treatment of this verse.[3]

17. JOHN 8:44

The difficulty attendant upon the determination of the antecedent of αὐτοῦ in the phrase ὅτι ψεύστης ἐστὶν καὶ ὁ πατὴρ αὐτοῦ leads Montgomery (p. 21) to render the phrase into Semitic idiom, where "the phrase would appear as 'the son of the lie and its father,' a drastically satirical utterance." Montgomery does not regard this as conclusive proof of translation, but Burrows (p. 125) feels that it is at least as good as any other explanation of this verse.

The Greek construction *ad sensum* is usually assumed by commentators and grammarians as adequate explanation of this passage.[4] Blass-Debrunner has a paragraph

---

[1] *Op. cit.*, I, 25.

[2] *Das Johannesevangelium, loc. cit.*   [3] *S. Jean, loc. cit.*

[4] Lagrange, *S. Jean, loc. cit.;* Winer-Moulton, *op. cit.*, p. 181; Bauer, *Das Johannesevangelium, loc. cit.*

on this construction with αὐτοῦ, and classifies this passage in John under that heading.

But this explanation of the pronoun is unnecessary, for, by simply referring the αὐτοῦ to the noun ψεῦδος which occurs earlier in the sentence, one secures a more natural Greek construction. The use of αὐτοῦ would seem, therefore, to be explicable on other grounds than recourse to Semitic idiom.

18. JOHN 8:25

The Greek of this passage, τὴν ἀρχὴν ὅτι καὶ λαλῶ ὑμῖν, seems to Montgomery (p. 21) "uncertain and absurd." He works out the following Aramaic original: "What was at first (*di bereshith*), what (*di*, represented by ὅτι) also I am saying to you," i.e., "I am saying the same thing as from the first.[1]

That this passage has been a stumbling-block to many and has been interpreted in many ways is not to be denied.[2] But treating the passage as a question or as an ironical exclamation eliminates the difficulties and has in its favor the consistent support of the Greek fathers. This is the interpretation supported by Winer-Moulton, Lagrange, Bauer, and others. It involves the use of ἀρχήν to mean ὅλως, a use which was quite common in classical Greek, usually with a negative.[3]

An instance of this use in Hellenistic Greek occurs in the papyri, P. Oxy. III, 472 (speech of an advocate, 130

---

[1] If the second *di* is represented by ὅτι, why is not the first *di*, which is in a parallel construction also represented by ὅτι?

[2] Cf. the commentaries of Lagrange and Bauer at this point.

[3] Bauer, *Wörterbuch*.

A.D.), lines 16 f.: οὐ δύναται γὰρ κεκλέφθαι τὸ μηδ' ἀρχὴν γενόμενον μὴ δυνατὸν δ' εἶναι . . . . , which the editors translate: "which neither ever existed at all nor could exist." Examples of this use without a negative are given in sufficient number in Bauer's commentary.

A weakness of Montgomery's conjecture lies in the fact that it requires the translation of a phrase which really means "from the beginning" by τὴν ἀρχήν. This is possible as Greek, but not probable in John, where ἀπ' ἀρχῆς is quite common.

The argument for mistranslation remains, then, here as elsewhere, without that convincing quality so to be desired for the demonstration of mistranslation.

19. John 4:6; 13:25: οὕτως

Montgomery (p. 21) mentions this "peculiar usage" rather to raise the question than to answer it. He suggests, however, that the answer may lie in an Aramaic original *kadu*, "as he was," used often in the Latin sense of *iam*. Torrey (p. 343) states his view more confidently: "In 4, 6 and 13, 25 οὕτως is simply the Jewish-Aramaic בְּכֵן 'therefore,' 'accordingly.' " In a later article[1] Montgomery repudiates his former suggestion and argues for the Aramaic original of οὕτως in these passages as being *wekadu*, "only." He finds an instance of this use in the fourteenth-century text of the *Life of Mar Yaballaha III*.[2]

Which of these conjectures best suits Aramaic usage

[1] "Some Aramaisms in the Gospels and Acts," *Journal of Biblical Literature*, XLVI (1927), 71-72.

[2] Burrows, *op. cit.*, p. 130, does not mention Montgomery's change.

may be left to the scholars in that field to determine;
that οὕτως as here used was good Greek usage is beyond
question. In classical Greek οὕτως was used in two somewhat similar ways to mean either "merely so," "as he
was," etc., or, after a participle, to take up again the idea
of the participle. Numerous examples of both are given
in Liddell and Scott, and in other lexicons and grammars;
e.g., Phaed. 61*d*: καὶ καθεζόμενος οὕτως ἤδη τὰ λοιπὰ διελέγετο; Aen. 6, 104: ἀποφυγὼν δὲ καὶ τούτους στρατηγὸς
οὕτω Ἀθηναίων ἀπεδέχθη.[1]

Walter Bauer asserts that if οὕτως were the pleonastic
reference to a preceding participle, it would have to precede the verb, citing Acts 20:11 and five other Hellenistic
passages in support of his claim. He concludes, therefore,
that οὕτως here is equivalent to ὡς ἁπλῶς and ὡς ἔτυχε.[2]
But that οὕτως need not always precede the verb when it
refers to a preceding participle is shown by the following
passage in Epictetus: ii. 8. 20: καὶ ἡ Ἀθηνᾶ ἡ Φειδίου
ἅπαξ ἐκτείνασα τὴν χεῖρα καὶ τὴν Νίκην ἐπ᾽ αὐτῆς δεξαμένη
ἕστηκεν οὕτως ὅλῳ τῷ αἰῶνι. . . . . Another instance of οὕτως
meaning "as he was" occurs in iv. 1. 116: πῶς δὲ πραθεὶς
ἀνεστρέφετο πρὸς τὸν δεσπότην· εὐθὺς διελέγετο πρὸς αὐτόν,
ὅτι οὐχ οὕτως ἐστολίσθαι δεῖ αὐτόν, οὐχ οὕτως κεκάρθαι. . . . ,
where Mrs. Carter translates "that he ought not to be
dressed or shaved in the manner he was."

Cadbury, in a study of this use of this word in Acts

[1] Quoted by Kühner-Gerth, *op. cit.*, § 486, 1, anm. 5. Cf. Winer-
Moulton, *op. cit.*, p. 772; Bauer, *Wörterbuch;* Pallis, *St. John and the
Apocalypse*, p. 8.

[2] *Das Johannesevangelium* on 4:6.

which shows (against Blass-Debrunner) that it need not be a mark of classical culture,[1] has shown its currency in the papyri. He quotes, with other examples, P. Lond. I, 106 (a complaint of assault, iii B.C.), line 19.

The conclusion seems inescapable that John's usage is paralleled in classical and Hellenistic Greek, and is in no sense "peculiar." Indeed, the difficulty in regard to this passage is caused by the fact that οὕτως was used so commonly and so freely that two slightly different constructions developed, both of which have been claimed by Greek scholars for John. A resort to Aramaic idiom is inadvisable in these circumstances.

MISTRANSLATIONS ALLEGED BY TORREY

Any detailed treatment of the "mistranslations" advanced by Torrey seems unnecessary in this study, since he himself admits (p. 344) that "in no one of the passages discussed is it necessary . . . . to postulate singular usage." Several of these passages, those in which Torrey picked the same passage as Burney or Montgomery, have already been discussed. In the other passages it may be worth while to note Lagrange's comment[2] on Torrey's suggestions.

In 11:33, 38, he claims a meaning for the Greek which would make Torrey's suggestion unnecessary, and points out that the error supposed by Torrey occurs twice in the same context, "qui suggérait plutôt l'émotion." In 7:3,

---

[1] "Lexical Notes on Luke-Acts. I," *Journal of Biblical Literature,* XLIV (1925), 223.

[2] Cf. his commentary at the various passages.

he rejects Torrey's conjecture as useless. In 14:2, he ignores it. In 14:31, he quotes Torrey's restoration with
the comment that it is very ingenious but much less
natural than the Greek. In 20:17, he regards the passage
as restored by Torrey as a redundance without meaning.
He ignores the three or four brief suggestions of mistranslations in Torrey's last paragraph—an example
which the author of this study feels justified in following
in view of their brevity, general insignificance, and non-
linguistic nature.

One of the mistranslations for which Torrey (pp. 341 f.)
argues at length, 14:31, deserves notice in connection
with his claim (p. 344) that in "no one of the passages is
it necessary to suppose carelessness or obtuseness on the
part of either copyist or translator." He reconstructs the
original Aramaic of the end of verse 31 as אֲקוּם וְאָזֵל
מִכָּה, and concludes that it was easy for the copyist to
write קוּמוּ נֵאזֵל מִכָּה which our Greek translates. Yet
he earlier (p. 329) took issue with Burney on the possibility of a translator mistaking מַעְיָן for מְעִין!

Burrows (p. 131) gives two additional mistranslations
suggested to him by Torrey in a letter: in 2:15 and 2:24
Torrey thinks πάντας mistranslates a neuter and that it
should therefore be πάντα. But in 2:15 he is attacking a
straw man, for the Greek text as it is means exactly what
he tries to make it mean by emendation.[1] And in 2:24
the meaning "all men" is much preferable to the "everything" that Torrey suggests, for the specific argument

[1] Cf. Goodspeed's and Weymouth's translations, and Alford's *Greek
Testament.*

of the context is that Jesus knew *people*. If Torrey had interpreted this verse by its immediate context instead of by a parallel in 21:17, which the author of the gospel probably did not write, he would have no reason for suggesting mistranslation.

It is interesting to note that as Torrey dealt with Burney's mistranslations, so has Lagrange dealt with Torrey's; and one would almost be justified in quoting Torrey's conclusion on Burney's attempts (p. 332) as an epitaph for Torrey's own work in this connection: "Among those who are inclined to demand in John what Burney demands in Mark (some cogent evidence of mistranslation), I think that the verdict is likely to be, 'Not proven.' "

CHAPTER V

CONCLUSIONS

The preceding chapters plainly indicate that those who claim that John's Greek is full of Aramaisms employ a method that is unscientific and present results that are consequently unconvincing. They use an inadequate control; they apply their own definitions and categories very inexactly; they rely on an especially weak use of the weakest of all linguistic weapons: the cumulative argument. In brief, their work is not characterized by that objectivity so essential to the demonstration of a hypothesis.

That the use of an adequate neutral control is necessary as a check upon linguistic theorizing was most brilliantly demonstrated by Professor Cadbury's study of the language of Luke.[1] Hobart, followed by an imposing group of New Testament scholars, claimed that Luke's language was medical because of its many agreements with the language of the Greek medical writers. Cadbury has conclusively demonstrated the weakness of this theory by setting up as a control the language of Greek writers who were not doctors and yet surpass Luke in the employment of these alleged medical terms. The long-continued vogue of the false idea that Luke's language was distinctly medical was possible only because no one before Cadbury attempted a control study. Hobart's main fault lay, not in his treatment of the writings of Luke or the

[1] *The Style and Literary Method of Luke* (Cambridge, 1919, 1920).

doctors, but in the fact that he failed to treat similarly writings where a negative result must be expected. This sin of omission is the most deadly that can be committed in any field of research. It invites the wildest flights of fancy, and permits superficial resemblances to masquerade as evidences of kinship. Thus an anthropologist, in trying to decide whether a recently excavated skeleton was that of a gorilla or a man, might decide that it was a gorilla because it had two legs, since he had often seen gorillas with two legs—unless he happened to notice his own legs in a mirror. Features common to gorillas and men cannot be used to distinguish one from the other; nor can constructions common to Aramaic and Greek serve as evidence of Aramaic influence upon a Greek document. The statement of Professor Burrows[1] that a construction which has been demonstrated to be current Greek usage is valueless as evidence of translation ought to lead those who are about to present us with another list of "Aramaisms" to first check up on current Greek usage.

No such check has been adequately employed by any of those who see extensive Aramaic influence upon John's Greek. Although Burney professes to employ the Synoptic Gospels as a pure(!) Greek check upon John, his actual divining rod is, "Does it look Semitic?" The same method is followed by the others, although they sometimes affirm that the usage under discussion is impossible as Greek, or point out that it occurs nowhere else in the New Testa-

[1] "The Original Language of the Gospel of John," *Journal of Biblical Literature*, XLIX, 98.

ment. This limitation of the Greek horizon to the pages of the New Testament would cripple any argument on the nature of its Greek, and is at the present day an almost unbelievable anachronism. Only when the whole range of Hellenistic Greek has been set beside the Fourth Gospel will its "Aramaisms" appear against a background which will make possible their proper evaluation. In order that the alleged Aramaisms of John may "look Semitic" to eyes which see but little Semitic literature, the Aramaic scholars must show that these constructions would not look Hellenistic to a Greek.

The method employed by these scholars reveals several defects which may be grouped together as lack of accurate and consistent definition. Burney, for example, urges a sharp distinction between Aramaisms and Hebraisms, but he employs both to further his argument. He claims that the passages where he finds "mistranslation" are characterized by difficulties and peculiarities of language, but in the discussion of more than one of these passages he speaks only of content and not at all of language. The Synoptics, he thinks, are Hellenistic Greek with which John may be contrasted; but, on the other hand, he thinks that they are very, very Semitic. Nor do these scholars limit themselves to that part of the Fourth Gospel which is generally regarded by New Testament scholars as coming from the pen of the author. Passages from the twenty-first chapter are quite frequently cited to strengthen their case, although this chapter is very generally regarded as an editorial addition to John; and Burrows actually employs the *pericope adulterae*, which is certainly not a part of the Fourth Gospel.[1] Such practices weaken rather than strengthen an argument.

Moreover, the main reliance of the plea for Aramaic influence upon the language of John is the "cumulative argument," an argument which accumulates through the hasty listing of usages which can on any pretext be classified as Semitic. This list is like the Hydra, as fast as study removes half a dozen usages, unchecked imagination replaces them with a dozen new Semitisms. Burrows' work may be taken as typical of the way in which the list of Aramaisms in John is kept long enough for an appeal to the cumulative argument to be possible. He removes from the list about a dozen usages which the work of Howard, Allis, and Driver established as Greek. To replace them he adds about a dozen usages which Burney, Montgomery, and Torrey did not include, or listed as unimportant.[2] One of the dozen is a passage from the *pericope adulterae* (see above), one is from the Synoptics! Incredible as it may seem, he includes (p. 119) 18:37, σὺ λέγεις ὅτι βασιλεύς εἰμι, as an Aramaism because he is able to quote a parallel from the Palestinian Talmud to the Synoptic phrase which has σὺ λέγεις alone. He fol-

[1] His evidences of "Thinking in Aramaic" (p. 117) include (22) 5:14 μηκέτι ἁμάρτανε with which he compares 8:11 πορεύου, ἀπὸ τοῦ νῦν μηκέτι ἁμάρτανε. He quotes a parallel to 8:11 from the Palestinian Talmud. The imperative with μηκέτι in 5:14 is obviously a link to connect the "Semitism" of 8:11 with the Fourth Gospel. The weakness of the link is shown by the fact that μηκέτι with an imperative occurs in Epictetus iv. 19. 9; Frag. 23. 19.

[2] Thus, one of his Aramaisms is taken from Montgomery's argument on the theology of the gospel.

lows (p. 117) Strack-Billerbeck in regarding the εὑρήκαμεν
of 1:45 as due to an Aramaic verb which could be translated "met"; but all the editors of BGU III, 846 (letter, ii
A.D.), lines 13 f., translate its use of this verb by "met"
without resource to an Aramaic original.[1] He follows (p.
116) Howard in adding as an Aramaism the phrase ὁ
υἱὸς τοῦ ἀνθρώπου, which probably was Aramaic in origin
but had become an established part of the Christian
vocabulary long before John was written. He admits
(p. 115), in regard to one of Montgomery's Semitisms,
that it is common to all languages and can consequently
have little value as evidence of Aramaic influence, but he
keeps it in the list. He rejects (p. 125) some of those mistranslations of Burney's which Torrey accepted, but he
quotes without adverse comment two of Torrey's later
"mistranslations" which do not merit serious consideration.[2] Nor is he any more critical in compiling his list of
"Biblicisms," for he includes here (p. 107) among other
good Greek constructions the cognate accusative, quoting
John 17:26 and 7:24.[3] The cumulative argument is already in bad odor with New Testament scholars because
of its employment in connection with the "medical"
language of Luke; its use in connection with a list of
Aramaisms in John compiled by the methods discussed
above is not likely to improve its reputation.

[1] Milligan, *Selections from the Greek Papyri* (Cambridge 1912) p. 94;
and Deissmann, *Light from the Ancient East*, p. 188, etc.

[2] See above, p. 121.

[3] Cf. Epictetus i. 29. 49 (quoted on p. 102); i. 16. 18; ii. 2. 10; iii. 26. 23;
iv. 1. 49, etc.; and any Greek grammar.

As might be expected from the fundamental defects in the method employed to secure them, the results of the Aramaic scholars' work are very unconvincing. The fact that they disagree as to what should be included in the list of Johannine Aramaisms is very significant. The majority of the 54 "Semitisms" discussed in chapters ii and iii were taken from the work of Burney and Montgomery, only 7 coming from Torrey's article. The work of Montgomery and Burney was done independently; and as each feels that the "Semitisms" which he advocates could not escape the notice of an Aramaic scholar, a comparison of their findings should be interesting. There are 29 "Semitisms" from Burney's list, and 22 from Montgomery's. Only two of these are duplicates! And the agreement is not even as high as that. In regard to one of these two, the use of the historical present, Burney is sure that its frequency is due to the Aramaic participle, but Montgomery is uncertain whether it is an Aramaism or good Greek usage. The extent of their agreement is that ὄνομα αὐτῷ is due to Semitic influence. It is ironic that their only agreement should be in error, for that ὄνομα αὐτῷ is a common construction in Hellenistic Greek is admitted by Burrows and has been demonstrated above.[1] The lack of agreement in these lists is an overwhelming indictment of the lists themselves and the method which produced them.

To give that convincing and final touch which the body of his argument lacked, Burney turned to the demonstration of mistranslation. Thirty "mistranslations" as sug-

[1] See pp. 34 f.

gested by Burney, Montgomery, or Torrey have been studied in chapter iv: 15 of Burney's, 5 of Montgomery's, 10 of Torrey's. In not a single one of these cases do all three agree in picking the same passage. Torrey repudiates Burney's list almost without exception, so that it is not surprising to find him disagreeing with Burney as to the original Aramaic in the two instances in which they pick the same passage. Burrows rejects Burney's list even more completely than Torrey does. Montgomery and Burney pick the same passage once, and give the same explanation for it. Montgomery and Torrey pick the same passage once, but disagree as to the original Aramaic; and Montgomery later disagrees with himself. Lagrange treats Torrey's mistranslations as Torrey treated Burney's, and, in general as in detail, feels that John's Greek does not read like translation from a Semitic original.[1] These disagreements further discredit the objectivity of the method which makes them possible.[2]

The 54 "Semitisms" in John taken from the work of Burney, Torrey, and Montgomery, which make the "cumulative argument" so enticing, fade away like snow in May when the bright light of Hellenistic Greek is turned upon them. Parallels to 40 of them have been given from Epictetus or the papyri, or both. Thirty-one of these "Semitisms" are adequately paralleled in classical Greek. Little more than half a dozen are left without adequate Greek parallel, and Christian writings composed in Greek contain parallels to most of these. Moreover, al-

[1] Lagrange, *S. Jean*, pp. cxvii–cxix.

[2] Cf. McNeile, *Introduction to New Testament* (Oxford, 1927), p. 278.

most all the passages where mistranslation is claimed have been paralleled in non-Christian Greek writings. If such a brief and narrow study of Hellenistic Greek as this one riddles the list of "Aramaisms" so thoroughly, what would happen if a comprehensive study were made? And in addition, it should be noted that Epictetus' agreements with John are much larger than this study may imply, for many a resemblance between them was passed over because that particular usage had not yet been claimed as an "Aramaism." With the abbreviated list of Aramaisms that remain, something qualitative and convincing is needed to bolster up the cumulative argument.[1]

For on the basis of the remnants of the lists of Burney, Montgomery, Torrey, and Burrows (and any other "Semitisms" which they have failed to notice),[2] nothing can be said against the present position of New Testament scholarship in regard to the Fourth Gospel. That is to say, what we find here is what would be expected of a gospel written in Greek at Ephesus about the year 100 A.D. by a Christian who knew some of the Synoptic Gospels in Greek (and perhaps the Septuagint also). We find nothing in the linguistic arguments advanced by these men which would be strange in such a gospel.

Finally, it may be well to reiterate the main points established. (I) The method employed by Burney and the other Aramaic scholars is unsound—for (1) they use

[1] See Cadbury's sound statement of this need elsewhere, *American Journal of Theology*, XXIV (1920), 445 f.

[2] Cf. Lagrange, *op. cit.*, p. cxvi, and Howard's Appendix to Moulton and Howard, *Grammar of New Testament Greek*, Vol. II.

no adequate control; (2) they are inaccurate and inconsistent; (3) they point to the cumulative force of a list of Aramaisms of the weakest sort. (II) Their results are not at all convincing: (1) they do not pick the same Aramaisms when they work independently; (2) they reject each other's mistranslations; (3) the vast majority (about 90 per cent) of their Aramaisms have been shown by this study to be paralleled in Greek; (4) what remains is the inevitable minimum of Semitisms in a gospel which inherited the earlier Christian traditions. There is here nothing to justify the claim that the author of the Fourth Gospel thought in Aramaic or wrote in Aramaic.

INDEXES

I. PERSONS AND SUBJECTS

Abbott, E. A. . . 18, 43, 77, 99, 104

Acts 81, 119

Acts of Thomas 14, 15

Adjective 75–81

Aelian 35

Aeneas 119

Aeschines 52

Aeschylus . . . 37, 38, 43, 72, 82

αἵματα 81–82

Allen, W. C. 64

ἀλλ' ἵνα 99

Allis, O. T.
   4, 6, 49, 67, 93, 94, 95, 98, 100, 105, 107, 108, 126

Andocides 38, 59

ἄνθρωπος 73–74

ἄνωθεν 43

Aorist indicative 68–71

Aorist participle, rarity of . 18–19

Apocalypse 35, 82, 94, 95

ἀποκρίνομαι 13, 14, 18

Apostolic Fathers 20

Appian 69, 70

Aristophanes 43, 72, 73

Aristotle 43, 73

Arrian 68

Artemidorus 43

Article, omission of 78–80

Asclepiodotus 47

Asyndeton 10–17

Asyndeton, in speeches . . . 12

Asyndeton, with ἀποκρίνομαι 13–14

Asyndeton, with λέγω . . 14–16

Asyndeton imperatives . . 16–17

Ball, C. J. 2, 108, 109

Barnes, W. E. . . . 6, 12, 54, 110

Bauer, Walter
   30, 33, 35, 37, 43, 44, 47, 57, 59, 75–77, 80–82, 84, 87, 88, 108, 112–14, 116–19

Bernard, J. H.
   14, 42, 44, 77, 87, 89, 99, 108, 112

Berthold, L. 1

Blass, Friedrich 31, 111

Blass-Debrunner
   55, 65, 66, 74, 76, 82, 84, 86, 99, 100, 113, 116, 120

Burkitt, F. C. 98

Burney, C. F.
   1, 2, 4, 5, 6, 8–11, 13, 14, 17–21, 25–27, 34–37, 46, 48–50, 52, 54, 55, 61, 63, 64, 68–71, 73, 74, 81, 86–89, 91, 92, 94–96, 98–109, 111, 114, 115, 120–22, 125–30

Burrows, M.
   5–7, 10, 16, 20, 27, 28, 31, 32, 36, 40, 42, 44, 46, 49, 51, 56, 58, 59, 61, 65, 71, 75, 77, 78, 81–83, 86, 97, 102, 109–11, 116, 118, 121, 124–26, 128–30

Burton, E. D. . . . 18, 42, 61, 63

Cadbury, H. J. 82, 119, 123, 130

Callimachus 47

Carter, Mrs. Elizabeth
   73, 97, 101, 102, 110, 119

Casus pendens 37–40

Change from direct to indirect
　discourse 113

Classical Greek
　21, 36, 37, 56, 60, 65, 75, 77, 84,
　93, 102, 103, 105, 115, 117, 119

Cognate accusative 127

Cognate dative 30–31

Conjunction 86–95

Construct state 78–80

Cumulative argument . . . 126

Dalman, G. . . . . viii, 2, 14, 31

δέ, infrequency of . . . 90–92

Deissmann, G. A. . . 33, 80, 127

Demosthenes 27, 43, 58, 62, 84, 116

Dick, K. 111

Diodorus Siculus . . . 47, 84, 109

Dionysius of Halicarnassus . 72

Driver, G. R.
　4, 6, 17, 26, 27, 46, 47, 51, 72,
　75, 98, 100, 108, 109, 126

Ebeling, H. 23, 52

εἰμί 58

εἰς τὰ ὀπίσω 83–84

ἐκ with genitive, used as nomi-
　native 86

ἐκεῖνος, *casus pendens* . . . 37

ἐκεῖνος, as a personal pronoun
　　　　　　　　　　　56–57

ἔλεγε (-ον) 29

ἔν, mistranslation of "this" 105–6

ἐν τοῖς Ἰουδαίοις, mistransla-
　tion of "in Judea" . . 115–16

Epictetus, *Discourses*
　7, 8, 9, 43, 56, 65, 90–93, 100,
　129, 130

Eratosthenes 77

ἔρχομαι 61

Euclid 88

Euripides 38, 43, 77, 82, 87, 88, 103

ἦν, mistranslation of "he" . . 107

Field, F. 43, 108

γάρ, infrequency of 92

Genesis 105

Genitive absolute, rarity of 19–21

Gildersleeve, B. L.
　16, 29, 37, 38, 41, 50, 52, 53, 58,
　60, 65, 76, 77, 82, 111, 115

"Go and do" for "continue to
　do" 32

Goguel, M. . . 97, 104, 109, 112

Goodwin, W. W.
　21, 29, 38, 61, 65, 71, 93, 105

Gray, G. B. 109

Halliday, W. R. 24

Harris, Rendel 110

Hebrew usage
　3, 14, 18, 22, 23, 26, 27, 35, 43,
　50, 57, 72, 81, 95, 103, 104, 125

Hermetic literature 33

Herodotus
　35, 38, 41, 43, 57, 60, 65, 68–70,
　87, 92, 105, 108, 116

Homer 28, 29, 37, 38, 50, 61, 63, 76

Howard, W. F.
　4–6, 17, 22, 23, 28, 31, 47, 48, 51,
　60, 65, 72, 73, 79, 80, 88, 95, 98,
　100, 101, 104, 105, 110, 114, 126,
　127, 130

Hultsch, F. 30

ἵνα 113

ἵνα, frequency of 92–93

ἵνα, mistranslation of "who" 96–99

ἵνα, mistranslation of "when"
　　　　　　　　　　99–100

ἵνα μή, frequency of . . . 93

ἵνα μή for μήποτε 94–95

Imperfect tense, mistranslation of pluperfect . . . 107–8
Isocrates 38, 75, 76, 116
ith, "there is" 58

James, M. R. 15
Jannaris, A. N.
28, 37, 48, 50, 84, 90, 92, 100
John the Baptist 107
καί, in speeches 17
καί, in narrative 18
καί, adversative 86–87
καί, introducing incredulous question 87–88
καί, "and so" 88–89
καταλαμβάνω, mistranslation of "darken" 108–9
Koine usage, variation in 6, 19, 20, 91
Kühner-Gerth
27, 29, 31, 35, 41, 47, 50, 56, 61, 62, 65, 76, 78, 81, 83, 84, 87, 88, 103, 111, 113, 119

Lagrange, M. J.
22, 25, 28, 38, 47, 54, 59, 63, 67, 68, 73, 80, 87, 88, 98, 100, 110, 114, 116, 117, 120, 122, 129, 130
Law, R. 72
λεγόμενος 40–41
λέγω . . 14, 15, 57–58, 65, 66, 70
Liddell and Scott
57, 73, 76, 89, 106, 119
"Living water" 44–45
Long, G. 110
Lucian 26, 27, 92
Lysias 62

Mandaean literature 33
Martyrdom of Polycarp . . 20
Mayser, E. 74, 83
McKenna, R. 60
McNeile, A. H. 81, 129

Medical language of Luke 123–24
Menander 25
μέσος, as a noun 75–76
Miller, C. W. E. 68
Milligan, G. . 33, 69, 70, 112, 127
Modern Greek
21, 48, 60, 90, 100, 101
Montgomery, J. A.
3, 6, 8, 16, 21, 24, 28, 30, 32, 33–36, 40, 42, 44, 51, 52, 55–59, 63–65, 77, 80–83, 86, 101, 115–18, 120, 126–30
Moulton, J. H.
6, 31, 33, 38, 47, 48, 52, 59, 60, 65, 69, 70, 72, 74, 77, 79, 86, 99, 111
Moulton and Howard . 69, 130
Moulton and Milligan
33, 58, 76, 84, 112
Mücke, R. 85

Negative adverbs 71–75
Noun 81–84

οἴδαμεν, mistranslation of "I know" 110–13
Oldfather, W. A. . . . 57, 58, 110
Olsson, B. . 44, 57, 62, 83, 74, 85
ὄνομα αὐτῷ 34–36
ὅπου . . . . ἐκεῖ 40
ὅς, mistranslation of "because" 104–5
ὅτε 20
ὅτι, mistranslation of "when" 100–101
ὅτι, mistranslation of "who" 101–2
οὐ μή . . . . εἰς τὸν αἰῶνα . 74–75
οὐκ ἄνθρωπος for "no one" . 73–74
οὖν 18, 88
οὖν, frequency of 89, 90
οὕτως, a mistranslation . 118–20

Pallis, A. 35, 60, 119

(πᾶν) ὅ, mistranslation of
"who" 103–4

πάντας, mistranslation of
"everything" 121

Papyri
7, 8, 9, 11, 19, 20, 23, 58, 90, 91,
92, 93, 94, 129

Parataxis 17–21

Partitive genitive 86

πᾶς μή, for "none" 71–73

Paul 75, 81

Pauline epistles 93, 94

Penick, D. A. 92

περί 84–86

Pericope adulterae . . . 125–26

Pernot, H.
21, 48, 87, 88, 90, 92, 98, 101,
108

Peshitto . . 49, 95, 98, 105, 115

Pindar 37

Place name followed by
"city," etc. 40–41

Plato
23, 37, 38, 43, 52, 57, 58, 60, 73,
76, 80, 82, 87, 88, 103, 116, 119

Plural verb with singular subject 36–37

Plutarch . . 18, 24, 27, 33, 35, 41

πνεῦμα 42–43

Polybius . . . 30, 65, 68, 69, 70

Preposition 84–86

Prologue 8, 11, 82

Pronoun, with copula and
predicate 33–34

Pronoun, demonstrative . 55–57

Pronoun, personal . . . 48–55

Pronoun, relative 46–48

Puns 42–43

Radermacher, L.
17, 31, 38, 47, 63, 72

ῥῆμα, mistranslation of "thing"
106–7

Rife, J. M. 22

Robinson, H. B. 20

Sallust 77

Schaeder, H. H. 82

Schenkl, H. . . 7, 39, 40, 53, 104

Schlatter, A. 1

Septuagint
5, 14, 20, 23, 25, 30, 31, 35, 44,
47, 48, 65, 67, 75, 80, 84, 86, 94,
98, 104, 106, 130

Sharp, D. S. 78, 85

Smyth, H. W. 58

"Son of . . . ." 80–81

Sophocles 16, 25, 26, 43, 59, 88, 103

Strack-Billerbeck 127

σύ 21, 22, 25

Subject, at end of sentence 24–25

Subject, after verb 21–23

Subject, now before, now after
verb 25

Superlative for comparative
degree 77–78

Synoptic Gospels
6, 7, 12, 14, 15, 18, 19, 20, 70,
80, 81, 89, 91–93, 112, 124, 126,
130

Syriac
24, 35, 94, 96, 98, 102, 105, 113

Syriac, Palestinian 48, 49, 50, 106

Tacitus 13

Thackeray, H. St. J.
30, 31, 47, 65, 67, 110

Theodotion . 13, 14, 64, 67, 106

Thinking in Aramaic 10, 36, 42, 81

Thucydides
28, 41, 43, 60, 62, 65, 68–70, 76,
87, 116

Torrey, C. C.
4, 6, 8, 19, 21, 22, 51, 52, 56, 75,

78–80, 84, 99, 107–11, 113, 118,
120–22, 126–30

ὕδατα 82–83
ὑπέρ 84–86
Upton, J. 110

Völker, F. 80
Verb, impersonal plural for
    passive 59–60
Verb, Semitic use of λέγω and
    εἰμί 57–59

Verb, tense 61–71
Verbal sequences 26–30
Wellhausen, J.
    2, 4, 20, 21, 23, 24, 51, 64, 75, 78
Weymouth, R. F. . . 68, 69, 70
Winer-Moulton
    27, 37, 38, 47, 71, 76, 77, 82,
    113, 116, 117, 119
Word order 21–25
Xenophon
    23, 28, 35, 37, 38, 46, 61, 65, 68,
    70, 76, 77, 86, 88, 113, 116

II. SOURCES

A. OLD TESTAMENT AND JEWISH

Genesis 6:17 47
Judges 7:4 57
I Kingdoms 67
I Samuel
    14:28 14
    19:22 14
II Chronicles
    29:31 14
    34:15 14
Ezra
    5:14 35
    5:15 32
    7:19–20 26
Psalm 35:10 44
Canticles 4:15 44
Isaiah
    1:21 48
    57:4 80
    66:10 31
Daniel
    Aramaic chapters
        13, 14, 22, 48, 64, 67, 71
    2:13 63
Joel 2:19 14
I Esdras 3:5 47
II Maccabees 12:37 47

B. NEW TESTAMENT

Matthew
    1:21 52
    3 10
    3 and 4 69
    10:26 97
    21:19 74
Mark
    1 . . . . 10, 69
    1:7 46
    3:29 74
    4:22 97
    11:14 74
Luke
    8 10
    8:17 97
    16:8 80
John
    1 . . . . . . 10, 48, 49
    1:4 104
    1:5 . . . . . . 87, 108
    1:6 . . . . . . 34, 46
    1:8 . . . . . 96, 97, 98
    1:9 107
    1:10 87
    1:12 . . . . . . 37, 38
    1:13 . . . . . 81, 104
    1:15 77

John

1:16	102
1:18	37
1:19—4:54	15
1:21*b*	25
1:27	46
1:29	61, 115
1:30	55
1:32	27
1:33	37, 46
1:39	26, 27
1:42	25
1:45	127
1:49	25, 78
2	11, 12
2:3	21
2:15	121
2:22	43, 107
2:24	121
3	11, 12
3:1	34, 46, 73
3:2	111
3:3	43
3:4	73
3:8	42
3:10	25
3:23	82
3:24	24
3:26	37
3:27	73, 74
3:28	55
3:29	30
3:31	115
3:32	37
4	11, 12
4—12	70
4:5	78
4:6	118
4:10, 11	44
4:14	44
4:19	25
4:47	29
5:7	73, 74, 96, 98
5:8	16
5:10	88
5:13	21
5:14	126
5:27	78
5:29	78

5:44	27
6	45
6:18	21
6:30	71, 96, 97, 98
6:37	103
6:39	103
6:50	96, 97, 98
6:51	45
6:53–59	115
6:57	88
6:63	106
6:66	83
6:68	78, 79, 106
6:70	57
7:3	120
7:23	73
7:24	127
7:37–38	109
7:38	44
7:42	40
7:46	73, 74
7:49	36
7:51	73
7:52	25
7:53—8:11	125, 126
8:11	126
8:12	33
8:21 f.	29
8:25	117
8:27	57
8:44	116
8:45	101, 102
8:48	25
8:56	113, 114, 115
9:5	78, 79
9:8	100
9:13	50
9:17	102
9:18	49, 50
9:25	106
9:36	46, 96, 97
10:17	54
10:24	29
10:27	54
10:28	54
10:29	103
11	10, 11, 12, 15
11:1	40
11:33	120

11:38 120
11:48 88
11:54 . . . . 40, 116
12:16 59
12:23 99
12:25 61
12:35 108
12:36 80
12:37 21
12:40 94
12:41 100
12:46 71
12:49 115
13:1 99
13:2 24
13:25 118
13:26 46
14:2 121
14:3 61
14:16 . . . . 96, 97
14:31 121
15:1 33
15:6 59
15:16 32
16:2 99
16:17 86
16:24 26
16:32 99
17:2 103
17:11 . . . . 87, 103
17:12 . . . . 80, 103
17:20 . . . . 61, 63
17:24 103
17:26 127
18 . . . . . . 10, 11, 12, 15
18:9 46
18:10 36
18:37 . . . . . . 25, 54, 126
19 . . . . 11, 12, 15
19:2 29
19:7 54
19:9 25
19:13–34 50
19:17 40
19:35 . . . . 56, 57
20:2 . . . . 59, 110
20:17 121
20:18 113
20:19 . . . . 21, 75

20:26 75
21:11 21
21:15–17 14
Acts
  2:47 63
  20:11 119
I Cor.
  4:1 73
  8:13 74
Eph.
  2:2 81
  5:6 81
Phil. 3:13 84
Col. 3:6 81
I Thess. 5:5 80
II Thess. 2:3 80
I John 5:4 104
Rev. 7:17 44

C. PATRISTIC

I Clement 21:9 48
Didache vii. 1, 2 44
Hermas *Shepherd* Vision
  1:1:3 83
  1:3:3 15
  3:2:4 . . . . 15, 83
  3:2:9 83
  3:3:5 83
  3:3:7 83
  3:6:1 81
  4:3:7 84

D. EPICTETUS

Discourses
  i. 1–24 89
  i. 1–11 . . . . 19, 20, 69, 70
  i. 1. 8 53
  i. 1. 12 112
  i. 1. 16 79
  i. 1. 28–30 66
  i. 2. 16 32
  i. 2. 18 . . . . . . 88, 89
  i. 3. 1 79
  i. 4. 2 89
  i. 4. 6 79

Discourses

i. 4. 10 79
i. 4. 13 53
i. 4. 15 . . . . . . 27, 32
i. 4. 29 27
i. 4. 32 60
i. 5. 3–5 111
i. 5. 4–5 87
i. 5. 6–10 111
i. 5. 9–10 53
i. 6. 9 40
i. 6. 32 40
i. 6. 37 111
i. 6. 38 112
i. 7. 24 87
i. 8. 3 39
i. 9. 10 53
i. 9. 21 39
i. 9. 27 89
i. 10. 6 34
i. 10. 7 . . . . . . 34, 53
i. 11. 32 87
i. 12. 1 59
i. 12. 5 59
i. 12. 6 59
i. 12. 15 24
i. 12. 30 24
i. 12. 31 53
i. 14. 10 39
i. 14. 24 . . . . . . 11, 12
i. 15. 3 24
i. 15. 4 59
i. 15. 5 27
i. 16. 11 17
i. 16. 18 127
i. 17. 3 24
i. 17. 12 79
i. 17. 18 99
i. 17. 28 62
i. 18. 4 27
i. 18. 13 f. 11
i. 18. 14 17
i. 19–ii. 5 15
i. 19–24 23
i. 19. 2 . . . . . . 34, 88
i. 19. 17 . . . . . . 24, 73
i. 19. 19 24
i. 19. 24 f. 11
i. 19. 27 62

i. 19. 28 . . . . 24, 27
i. 20. 14 27
i. 22. 5 76
i. 22. 15 59
i. 24. 3 . . . . . . 53, 97
i. 24. 5 . . . . . . 17, 32
i. 24. 13 39
i. 24. 19 89
i. 25. 2 39
i. 25. 8 . . . . 16, 17, 24
i. 25. 18 62
i. 25. 24 . . . . . . 24, 39
i. 25. 30 17
i. 25. 32 24
i. 26—ii. 16 66
i. 26—ii. 15 71
i. 26. 12 66
i. 27. 1 . . . . . . 28, 87
i. 27. 2 39
i. 27. 6 17
i. 27. 9 17
i. 27. 17 . . . . . . 24, 34
i. 28 (title) 74
i. 28. 10 74
i. 28. 20 26
i. 29. 4–6 15
i. 29. 10 17
i. 29. 11 88
i. 29. 16 58
i. 29. 18 57
i. 29. 21 24
i. 29. 27 62
i. 29. 42 24
i. 29. 47 25
i. 29. 49 . . . . . 102, 127
i. 29. 52 39
i. 29. 58 24
i. 29. 61 27
i. 29. 64 39
i. 29. 65 66
i. 30. 1 43
i. 30. 6–7 112
ii. 1. 2 24
ii. 1. 24 39
ii. 1. 35 . . . . . . 17, 27
ii. 2. 10 127
ii. 2. 20 26
ii. 2. 21 39
ii. 2. 25 27

ii. 5. 12	. . . .	39
ii. 5. 20	. . . .	85
ii. 5. 21	. . . .	39
ii. 6. 8	. . . .	57
ii. 6. 20	. . . .	105
ii. 6. 22	. . . .	39
ii. 7. 11	. . . .	39
ii. 7. 13	. . . .	16
ii. 8. 4	. . . .	58
ii. 8. 11	. . . . . .	34, 57
ii. 8. 13	. . . .	58
ii. 8. 20	. . . .	119
ii. 8. 25	. . . .	27
ii. 10. 12	. . . .	36
ii. 10. 23	. . . .	39
ii. 12. 4	. . . .	27
ii. 12. 11	. . . .	39
ii. 12. 15	. . . .	27
ii. 12. 20	. . . .	58
ii. 13. 1	. . . .	73
ii. 13. 5	. . . .	73
ii. 13. 9	. . . .	85
ii. 13. 14	. . . .	39
ii. 13. 18	. . . .	85
ii. 14. 3	. . . .	103
ii. 14. 21	. . . . . .	87, 101
ii. 15. 18	. . . .	102
ii. 15. 20	. . . .	24
ii. 16. 16	. . . .	30
ii. 16. 20	. . . .	27
ii. 16. 37	. . . .	39
ii. 16. 44	. . . .	110
ii. 17. 27	. . . .	43
ii. 17. 33	. . . .	34
ii. 18. 3	. . . .	27
ii. 18. 31	. . . .	101
ii. 18. 32	. . . .	100
ii. 19. 20	. . . .	27
ii. 19. 29	. . . .	34
ii. 19. 34	. . . .	27
ii. 20. 4	. . . .	27
ii. 20. 23	. . . .	59
ii. 20. 26	. . . .	17
ii. 21. 4	. . . .	39
ii. 21. 11	. . . .	88
ii. 21. 17	. . . .	39
ii. 21. 18	. . . .	39
ii. 22. 1	. . . .	39
ii. 22. 3	. . . .	39
ii. 22. 9	. . . .	27
ii. 22. 10	. . . .	27
ii. 22. 14	. . . .	76
ii. 22. 23	. . . .	76
ii. 22. 33	. . . .	76
ii. 23. 39	. . . .	39
ii. 24. 3	. . . .	39
ii. 24. 29	. . . .	27
ii. 26. 7	. . . .	27
iii. 1. 4	. . . .	39
iii. 1. 12	. . . .	51
iii. 1. 20	. . . .	102
iii. 1. 22	. . . . . .	25, 40
iii. 1. 23	. . . .	34
iii. 1. 37	. . . .	102
iii. 1. 44	. . . .	39
iii. 3. 8	. . . .	39
iii. 3. 15	. . . .	76
iii. 5. 2	. . . .	25
iii. 5. 3	. . . .	17
iii. 5. 5	. . . .	109
iii. 5. 11	. . . .	109
iii. 7. 4	. . . .	78
iii. 7. 24	. . . .	78
iii. 9. 13	. . . .	76
iii. 9. 22	. . . .	27
iii. 12. 15	. . . .	17
iii. 13. 21	. . . .	17
iii. 14. 3	. . . .	17
iii. 15. 6	. . . .	104
iii. 17. 1	. . . .	27
iii. 20. 12	. . . .	27
iii. 21. 5	. . . .	17
iii. 21. 6	. . . . . .	17, 32
iii. 22. 5	. . . . . .	32, 34
iii. 22. 6	. . . .	34
iii. 22. 55	. . . .	76
iii. 22. 76	. . . .	58
iii. 22. 88	. . . .	34
iii. 23. 12	. . . .	32
iii. 24. 81	. . . .	94
iii. 24. 85	. . . .	17
iii. 24. 102	. . . .	59
iii. 24. 114	. . . .	57
iii. 24. 117	. . . .	51
iii. 26. 22	. . . .	17
iii. 26. 23	. . . .	127
iii. 26. 39	. . . .	27
iv. 1. 8	. . . .	34

Discourses

iv. 1. 46	24
iv. 1. 47	62, 76
iv. 1. 49	127
iv. 1. 51	26, 79
iv. 1. 66	58
iv. 1. 73	30
iv. 1. 77	39
iv. 1. 82–83	85
iv. 1. 99	39, 58
iv. 1. 106	17
iv. 1. 108	97
iv. 1. 116	119
iv. 1. 132	62
iv. 1. 134	50
iv. 1. 154	24
iv. 1. 166	24
iv. 1. 168	24
iv. 1. 173	71
iv. 1. 177	24
iv. 2. 4	24
iv. 2. 8	17
iv. 3. 3	39
iv. 3. 9	98
iv. 4. 15	17, 40
iv. 5. 2	24
iv. 5. 9	24
iv. 5. 20	24
iv. 5. 24	76
iv. 5. 28	40
iv. 6. 5	39
iv. 6. 16	40
iv. 7. 13	27
iv. 7. 14	40
iv. 7. 18	27
iv. 7. 20	51
iv. 7. 21	102
iv. 7. 31	34
iv. 7. 36	40
iv. 8. 15	34
iv. 8. 16	34
iv. 8. 17–20	69
iv. 8. 22	24
iv. 8. 24	24
iv. 8. 25	34
iv. 8. 26	34
iv. 8. 37	25
iv. 9. 11	17
iv. 10. 5	102

iv. 10. 14	39
iv. 11. 17	17
iv. 11. 21	60
iv. 11. 23	102
iv. 11. 25	40
iv. 11. 34	32
iv. 12. 16	36
iv. 13. 4	94
iv. 13. 11	34
iv. 13. 15	17, 27
iv. 19. 9	126

Encheiridion 51 98

Fragments 23. 19 126

E. PAPYRI

P. Oxy(rhynchus)

I, 33	16, 88
I, 34	79
I, 37	79
I, 40	26
I, 41	75, 76
I, 99	41
I, 106	89
I, 113	11, 54, 62, 102
I, 117	47
I, 119	60, 75
II, 244	63
II, 245	63
II, 249	41
II, 254	41
II, 268	39
II, 281	51
II, 294	54
II, 295	16
II, 298	54, 112
II, 299	39
III, 465	36, 59
III, 466	11
III, 472	66, 69, 117
III, 474	89
III, 480	49
III, 498	49
III, 508	78
III, 513	50
III, 526	69
III, 528	62
III, 531	26
IV, 736	79

VI, 886	. . . .	26
VI, 918	. . . .	41
VI, 930	. . . .	30
VI, 933	. . . .	85
VI, 939	. . . .	109
VII, 1061	. . . . . .	112
VIII, 1162	. . . . . .	31
IX, 1188	. . . .	19
IX, 1216	. . . .	54
X, 1291	. . . .	62
X, 1294	. . . . . .	26, 94
XII, 1409	. . . . . .	83
XII, 1427	. . . . . .	83
XII, 1479	. . . . . .	112
XII, 1481	. . . . . .	112
XIV, 1647	. . . . . .	79
XIV, 1672	. . . . . .	71
XIV, 1761	. . . . . .	112

B(erlin) G(riechische) U(rkunden)

I, 19	. . . .	38
I, 38	. . . .	87
I, 139	. . . .	41
I, 217	. . . .	41
I, 282	. . . .	78
II, 372	. . . .	38
II, 384	. . . .	87
II, 385	. . . .	39
II, 388	. . . .	76
II, 423	. . . .	102
II, 449	. . . .	112
II, 511	. . . .	34
II, 523	. . . .	38
II, 531	. . . .	74
II, 595	. . . .	44
III, 846	. . . . . .	28, 127
IV, 1035	. . . .	63
IV, 1041	. . . .	62
IV, 1079	. . . .	34
IV, 1081	. . . .	114

P. Lond(on)

I, 106	. . . .	120
II, 142	. . . .	103
II, 177	. . . .	51
II, 262	. . . .	31
II, 265	. . . .	11, 16
II, 289	. . . .	41
II, 306	. . . .	62, 63
II, 328	. . . .	24
II, 331	. . . .	112
II, 358	. . . .	41
III, 897	. . . .	57
III, 1177	. . . .	83

P. Teb(tunis)

II, 272	. . . .	59
II, 278	. . . .	87
II, 283	. . . .	88
II, 311	. . . .	41
II, 374	. . . .	50
II, 382	. . . .	41
II, 408	. . . .	85
II, 412	. . . .	62

P. Fay(um)

106	. . . .	51
108	. . . .	76
117	. . . . .	11, 26, 37, 60
127	. . . .	39

Bib(liothèque)Nat(ionale)

Suppl. gr. 514	. . . . .	36
Suppl. gr. 574	. . . . .	33

P. Strassb(urg) II, 1173 . . 63

P. Giess(en) 17 114

P. Ryl(ands)

II, 113	. . . .	72
II, 153	. . . .	28

P. Petr(ie)

II, 18	. . . .	84
III, 23	. . . .	84

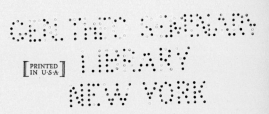

5489-1
119